WITH HOPE IN YOUR HEART:

A HILLSBOROUGH SURVIVOR'S STORY, THE DENIAL OF JUSTICE & A PERSONAL BATTLE WITH PTSD

by

Christopher Whittle

A Bright Pen Book

Copyright © Christopher Whittle 2012

British Library Cataloguing Publication Data.
A catalogue record for this book is available from the British Library

ISBN 978-0-7552-1478-5

Authors OnLine Ltd
19 The Cinques
Gamlingay, Sandy
Bedfordshire SG19 3NU
England

This book is also available in e-book format, details of which are available at www.authorsonline.co.uk

About the Author

Christopher Whittle is a survivor of the Hillsborough Disaster, and a lifelong Liverpool fan, working tirelessly for the quest for JUSTICE FOR THE 96. He holds a Combined Honours degree in Education Studies with History from the University of Central Lancashire, and is married to Deborah, with two grown up step-children and two cats called Pixie & K-Leb.

Christopher is a member of the Burnley & District Writers Circle.

He is a committed and practising Roman Catholic, involved in many aspects of parish life. He has worked in schools as a Teaching Assistant, and also writes fiction under the pseudonym of Christopher Corcoran.

Acknowledgements

I would like to acknowledge the following people, without them this work would never had been done:

Firstly, I would like to thank my loving wife Deborah, forever tasting sweet like wine. She has supported me through thick and thin, been totally loyal and has had to put up with an awful lot. I owe her a great debt and gratitude.

I would also like to say thank you for everything to my parents, Robert & Genevieve Whittle, who have been there for me, supported me, and helped me throughout my life. Without their amazing support, I would have achieved absolutely nothing. They are the best parents that anyone could ever wish for.

Also, my late Grandparents Henry and Mary Corcoran, as well as my family in Leyland - Anne, John, Mandy & Luis - and a special mention to my late Auntie Nancy, who always believed in me. A mention to my two cats, Pixie & K-Leb too!!!

I offer great gratitude and love to my stepchildren Zachary and Kendra. It has been a rocky road at times, but I hope that I taught you so much, just as I have learnt from you. I would also like to offer thanks to my extended family, who taught me so much about kindness, generosity and family love. I offer this to my in-laws, Paul and Doris, to my brother –in-law Andrew and his wife, Rachel, to my brother-in-law, Anthony and his wife, Christine, to my sister-in-law, Frances, and her husband, Gary, and to my sister-in-law, Angela, and her husband, Bryan. A thank you also goes to Deborah's aunt and uncle, Andrew and Sheila. I could not forget all my nieces and nephews, who bring me so much joy – so Ella, Eva, George, Kate, Josh, Noah, Millie & Lianna BIG HUGS.

I also dedicate this work to my late brother, Anthony. You'll Never Walk Alone

To my RED FAMILY, without you none of this would have been possible. There are far too many people to mention, if I miss you out then I am sorry. A special mention must go to Anne Williams, who is a true inspiration. I would also like to thank the HILLSBOROUGH JUSTICE CAMPAIGN & HOPE FOR HILLSBOROUGH who have helped me come to terms with PTSD. I would also like to thank Dean Harris, and a few of the BURNLEY REDS – Mick, Eric, John and Steve, as well as everyone in the Albert on matchdays!!! A special mention also goes to the HJC shop and to Gerry, Debi and all of the gang.

I would also like to thank my FACEBOOK friends, especially Rose Falconer, Hayley Barber, Jeni Barton, Steve Hart, Daniel MacArthur, John Lemmon, and so many, many more. A special thank you to Father Michael Waters, and all of the parishioners at Saint John the Baptist Roman Catholic Church, Burnley, and especially the Bereavement Ministry Team and the Journey in Faith Programme.

Of course, this would not be complete without paying tribute to the bereaved families and the survivors of the Hillsborough Disaster. This book is dedicated to them and to the 96 angels who lost their lives at Hillsborough:

John Alfred Anderson 62
Colin Mark Ashcroft 19
James Gary Aspinall 18
Kester Roger Marcus Ball 16
Gerard Bernard Patrick Baron 67

Simon Bell 17
Barry Sidney Bennett 26
David John Benson 22
David William Birtle 22
Tony Bland 22
Paul David Brady 21
Andrew Mark Brookes 26
Carl Brown 18
David Steven Brown 25
Henry Thomas Burke 47
Peter Andrew Burkett 24
Paul William Carlile 19
Raymond Thomas Chapman 50
Gary Christopher Church 19
Joseph Clark 29
Paul Clark 18
Gary Collins 22
Stephen Paul Copoc 20
Tracey Elizabeth Cox 23
James Philip Delaney 19
Christopher Barry Devonside 18
Christopher Edwards 29
Vincent Michael Fitzsimmons 34
Thomas Steven Fox 21
Jon-Paul Gilhooley 10
Barry Glover 27
Ian Thomas Glover 20
Derrick George Godwin 24
Roy Harry Hamilton 34
Philip Hammond 14
Eric Hankin 33

Gary Harrison 27

Stephen Francis Harrison 31

Peter Andrew Harrison 15

David Hawley 39

James Robert Hennessey 29

Paul Anthony Hewitson 26

Carl Darren Hewitt 17

Nicholas Michael Hewitt 16

Sarah Louise Hicks 19

Victoria Jane Hicks 15

Gordon Rodney Horn 20

Arthur Horrocks 41

Thomas Howard 39

Thomas Anthony Howard 14

Eric George Hughes 42

Alan Johnston 29

Christine Anne Jones 27

Gary Philip Jones 18

Richard Jones 25

Nicholas Peter Joynes 27

Anthony Peter Kelly 29

Michael David Kelly 38

Carl David Lewis 18

David William Mather 19

Brian Christopher Matthews 38

Francis Joseph MacAllister 27

John McBrien 18

Marian Hazel McCabe 21

Joseph Daniel McCarthy 21

Peter McDonnell 21

Alan McGlone 28

Keith McGrath 17

Paul Brian Murray 14

Lee Nicol 14

Stephen Francis O'Neill 17

Jonathon Owens 18

William Roy Pemberton 23

Carl William Rimmer 21

David George Rimmer 38

Graham John Roberts 24

Steven Joseph Robinson 17

Henry Charles Rogers 17

Andrew Sefton 23

Inger Shah 38

Paula Ann Smith 26

Adam Edward Spearritt 14

Philip John Steele 15

David Leonard Thomas 23

Patrick John Thompson 35

Peter Reuben Thompson 30

Stuart Paul William Thompson 17

Peter Francis Tootle 21

Christopher James Traynor 26

Martin Kevin Traynor 16

Kevin Tyrell 15

Colin Wafer 19

Ian David Whelan 19

Martin Kenneth Wild 29

Kevin Daniel Williams 15

Graham John Wright 17

JUSTICE FOR THE 96
JUSTICE FOR THE FAMILIES
JUSTICE FOR THE SURVIVORS
YOU'LL NEVER WALK ALONE

CONTENTS

Preface

THE HILLSBOROUGH DISASTER on 15TH of April 1989 is painfully etched on the memories of the bereaved families, the survivors, all Liverpool fans, former players, and indeed anyone with any connection to Liverpool Football Club. It is a disaster unique in British history. A total of 96 men, women and children lost their lives when they were crushed to death at the FA Cup semi-final between Liverpool and Nottingham Forest at the Hillsborough Stadium, Sheffield. The root causes of the disaster, as featured in The Taylor Report, was that of gross police mismanagement, and lack of care and control.

So why was this disaster unique?

It was unique due to the lies, fabrications, accusations, cover ups, coercion, suppression of evidence and deliberate falsehoods by sections of successive governments, the media, writers, politicians, ill-informed members of the public, the then coroner, and senior officers within the South Yorkshire Police force and West Midlands Police. After all, in no other disaster has the survivors, and indeed, those that lost their lives, been blamed for what occurred. What occurred that sunny April afternoon in Sheffield was shocking to the extreme. Furthermore, 23 years on, the families and the survivors are still fighting for JUSTICE FOR THE 96.

This account has been written by one such survivor, who was in the middle of the horrific crush in Pen 4 of the Leppings Lane terrace. I was injured that day physically and psychologically, and I still show the emotional scars today.

I will tell fully, in graphic detail what happened that fateful day at Hillsborough. I will tell fully of the immediate aftermath and the shocking treatment of survivors and loved ones. I will tell fully of the seemingly endless, almost a quarter of a century, quest for JUSTICE.

I have often noticed that no book has ever been written about Hillsborough, from the eyes of a survivor, and certainly not from anyone who was in the central pens of Leppings Lane – Pens 3 & 4. I felt it was time that this was addressed.

This is MY story of Hillsborough and how it has controlled my life for 23 years. It is something which I thought that I would never be able to write, and it is, without doubt, the most difficult thing I have ever had to undertake. Anyone who knows what PTSD or Post Traumatic Stress Disorder does to a person will understand what I mean. I therefore thank God in giving me the courage to do so.

I will tell a little about my life, what it was to be a Liverpool supporter in the 1980's. What it was like to follow the best team in Europe, the horrors of Heysel, and of course, the main focus of this book, the Hillsborough Disaster, the 15th of April 1989, and the aftermath, and the year of total injustice and blatant cover ups.

I will also tell of the last 23 years, and my battle with Post Traumatic Stress Disorder. I will tell of the second tragedy that was to befall me, the death of my brother, Anthony, and how it profoundly affected both me and my family. I will also tell how I turned my life around and what 23 years later, my life is actually like.

Chapter One

Born to be a Scouse

My family history is a complicated, rich and varied one, and like many Liverpudlian's its roots were firmly developed in the Irish Republic. I know for a fact that my family on my mother's side, the Corcoran's, came to Liverpool in the late 1800's. Of course there was no Republic back then, but what there was was rife poverty, inequality, illness, disease and little or no work. A familiar story I hear you cry. It kind of reminds me of Thatcher's Britain during the 1980's, where there was an almost obsessive destruction of the working class, and pretty much like what Cameron's Britain is becoming.

My great grandfather settled in Liverpool and worked on the docks, before ending up in Ormskirk, My grandfather was born in the Lancashire market town, on the Merseyside border, in 1902. The family later had a farm near Skelmersdale. My grandfather, Henry Corcoran, married Mary McGrath, whose family had also come from Ireland. She lived in the small West Lancashire town of Leyland, famous for it's trucks and the factories that made them. My Mum was born there in November 1927. Both my grandparents worked in the factories during the war making ammunitions and building tanks for the war effort.

After the war, a move further away from Liverpool was on the cards. It came to fruition in the late 1940's, really for employment reasons. So the Corcoran's moved to the industrial cotton and mining town of Burnley. Eventually, my Mum married my Dad, Robert Whittle, in March 1952. My father was a chief draughtsman for the National Coal Board at Bank Hall Colliery in Burnley. He later became a teacher of Woodwork & Technical Drawing in High School. It certainly had become quite a journey for the Corcoran's over the years from Ireland to Burnley, via Liverpool, Ormskirk, Skem and Leyland!!!

I was born on the 24th of June 1961, thus becoming a Burnley lad. But that is not the whole story. I was a Liverpool fan, a Red, from as long as I can remember. I was about 4 years old. The mid sixties was a great time to be in Liverpool, so I was told. The Beatles ruled the world, musically, and Liverpool were just about the best team around, winning the league championship in 1964, the FA Cup Final in 1965, and the league title again in 1966, under the managership of the legend that was the mercurial Bill Shankly. A man, you could say who, re-created Liverpool Football Club. A man who brought them up from the brink of near extinction at the bottom of the old second division to the greatest team in England. The European Cup should have been theirs too, in 1965. The infamous Inter Milan tie, who were supposed to be the best club side in the world at that time, came to Anfield in the semi final and were soundly beaten 3 – 1 in the first leg. One of those great Anfield European nights that have been famous over many a year since. Some older fans say it was the greatest European night ever at Anfield. The second leg was a dubious affair, with blatant refereeing decisions going against Liverpool in favour of Inter Milan. Ask Tommy Smith. Without any shadow of a doubt, The Reds were cheated out of a place in the final. We would have to wait another 12 years before getting to a European Cup Final, when 'Sir' Bob Paisley took his brilliant side to Rome and triumphed 3 – 1 over Borussia Moenchengladbach. Yet, before that glorious night in the eternal city happened, Liverpool would appear in three other European Finals, in the UEFA Cup and the European Cup Winners Cup. In 1966, the Reds lost again, in the European Cup Winners Cup Final at Hampden Park to Borussia Dortmund, despite overwhwelming support in Glasgow that night. There would be a wait of seven years before finally Liverpool secured a European trophy, the UEFA Cup in 1973, coupled with another league title. Shanks had conquered Europe. This feat would be repeated again, in 1976, under the managership of the late, great Bob Paisley.

By this time I was a very impressionable teenager. I had seen Liverpool play a few times during my early years, but my Dad, a lifelong Burnley fan, tried to influence me to the Claret and Blue faith at temple Turf Moor. As I got older, I was to have none of that. By the age of 16, I was regularly attending matches at Anfield. There was to be only one faith, in footballing terms, one church, one cathedral, one holy altar, and that was Anfield and The Mighty Red Men, Liverpool FC. Indeed, I was destined from such a young age, to have a LIVERBIRD UPON MY CHEST.

Chapter Two

A Liver Bird Upon My Chest – personal football stories

By the time I was regularly travelling to watch Liverpool, both home and away, from about 1977, football hooliganism was rife in this country, although it had not yet reached it's peak. It had started to rear it's ugly head in the late 1960's with Millwall being the first club in the country to witness it. Hardly a great surprise given their fans' record over the years. As we entered the 1970's, other fans from other clubs got involved, most notably Manchester United, Chelsea, West Ham and Leeds United. Yet, it was to get much, much worse.

I travelled to games at Anfield in those days by train. It was an early start, change at Preston, and catch the service to Ormskirk. I always loved the Preston – Ormskirk line, with beautiful views of the West Lancashire countryside – I am beginning to sound like a travel writer!!! It was then all change for the Merseyrail service to Liverpool Central. Although, I soon found out that others travelling for the match often got off at Kirkdale, so I followed suit. It was a great day out watching the Reds, often sampling some hostelries along the route to Anfield, the first port of call being the old Railway pub just outside Kirkdale station. Sadly it did not last long and closed in the late 1970's, replaced by a new pub just a few yards down the road, called The Peacock, which still stands today. Then it was off to the likes of The Melrose Abbey, The Stanley (which later became The Sportsman, part owned by Liverpool and Ireland legend, Ronnie Whelan). Sadly, it is now closed, replaced by an housing development. A little further down the road was The Elm Tree, built in 1978. Regrettably, it's now a 'bluenose' pub!!! Others worth a mention are The Clock, a pub named The Pacific, which has now changed it's name and The Barlow Arms. Obviously, I would not sample each pub en route or I would have been bladdered by the time the game started!!! I am just giving you a sample of what was on offer. As you got nearer the ground you could smell the addictive atmosphere, even several hours before kick off. I would walk past the Stanley Park railings and up the hill towards Anfield Road, just passing the King Harry pub – or sometimes not passing!!! As you turned the corner you faced a cobbled back street. At the top end of that back street was the view of the famous, world renowned, old Spion Kop, the most famous standing terrace in world football. It was built in 1906 and is named after the Battle of Spion Kop in Natal, South Africa, which occurred during The Boer War. Many other clubs followed Liverpool's lead and built a Spion Kop to house their nosiest supporters. Yet the Spion Kop at Anfield is unique in world football. At it's peak it housed something like 28,000 fans, though this was gradually reduced over the years. It is now an all seater stand with a capacity of just 12,000. As you got nearer there was a certain buzz, street sellers trying to sell their wares – "Hats, caps, scarves, badges or your t shirts," they would cry in that magnificent Scouse accent so full of character and that famous, world renowned wit. What a time it was to be a Liverpool fan. A team of legends who would die for the shirt, I only wish that was the case today. A great manager in Bob Paisley, in my eyes the greatest. In Kenny Dalglish the greatest Red there has ever been. No question. The fans, the very best in the whole world. The great pre match singalongs in the famous Albert pub, the Park too. And off to the chippy at a quarter to three for curry and chips. Oh absolute heaven. What wonderful, memorable days.

I became a Kopite in 1977 when I was 16 years old. Although, I occasionally watched the game from other parts of the ground, most notably the Paddock and the 'Anny Road End.' Here, I would hear the endless cries of 'We're da barmy Anny Road Army.' It was, however, pretty much the Kop for me and I was saved from the pure mental torture of the Boys Pen. I have heard stories of this area of the ground that would make the eyes water of the hardest of men. If Charles Darwin had written his idea of 'the survival of the fittest' in the Boys Pen then he could not have gone wrong. You could describe it as living in purgatory, before entering into Heaven, otherwise known as the Spion Kop. Others might describe the Boys Pen, however, as living in Hell. It was your apprenticeship before you graduated and became a Kopite. If you could survive the Boys Pen, then you could survive absolutely anything.

I travelled up and down the country throughout the late 1970's and all through the 1980's – visiting some weird and wonderful places, in various competitions, like Stockport County, Carlisle United, York City – now that has to be the best town in the land for a good bevy!!! The two cup ties against them back in 1986 & 1987 were great occasions, and they gave us a good game twice in consecutive seasons, needing a replay at Anfield both times. In fact, in 1986, they nearly knocked us out as we needed extra time to beat them at home. The cup competitions were great in the sense that we were able to visit places that we would not normally get the opportunity to do. In the league, we would regularly visit Everton, Manchester United, Manchester City, Leeds United, Arsenal, Tottenham, Chelsea, Aston Villa, Birmingham City, Nottingham Forest and the like. In some ways it would get boring after endless visits!!! My favourite away trip in the league though has to be Watford. A lot might be surprised by that statement, but during the height of football hooliganism in the early to mid eighties, I always found the Watford fans to be fair minded, friendly and with not one hint of trouble. We would have a good bevy or three with them and a good laugh. I don't know if any fellow Reds can recall a pub in Watford called The One Crown, a short ten minute walk to the Vicarage Road ground. We had some great times in there!!!

On the other side of the coin, I have been to some right shitholes as regards football grounds, and that is where the old chant by Liverpool fans comes from – 'shitty ground.' We were penned in like caged animals and treated like crap, as most football fans were. Some of the smaller grounds were the worst, such as Oxford United and Luton Town, but the ultimate in awful grounds had to be The Dell at Southampton. What a shithole of an away end that was. If I can recall, I think it was called the Archer Road Terrace. It was tight, small, claustrophobic, and the view was awful – you needed the neck of a giraffe to see absolutely anything!!! I am sure others can concur.

The 1980's were a time of great change, not always for the better. Certainly not with the government that we had in 'power' at that time – an abuse of power would be a more apt description. The evils of Thatcherism, a right wing, laissez-faire ideology of the rich getting richer, the poor getting poorer, a crazy notion of 'I'm alright Jack, sod the rest,' the thought that greed is good, a virtual fascist police state, the gradual decay and erosion of community spirit and morals, mass unemployment, especially in the north, the destruction of manufacturing industry, abject poverty. It was a time of rebellion, of inner city riots, of trying to find something to cling to. It was a time of a terrible, uncaring government, but great music, TV and cinema, and fantastic, out of this world football. We had to have something to believe in, especially on Merseyside, and we believed in football, and our wonderful team provided that belief. Was there a connection between the problems of 1980's Britain and the rise and rise of football hooliganism? I think many sociologists and social commentators believe so and to a certain extent I hold to that theory too.

The continued growth of football hooliganism throughout the 1980's focused the minds of the Tory right. It was no secret that Thatcher hated football and wanted to destroy it. It is certainly true that the yob element in this country brought great shame on the beautiful game and certainly their actions cannot be condoned, but to the Thatcher government, it became an obsession for them to try to destroy football any way they could. Certainly, the facilities for football fans were quite appalling. It would have been a better idea, therefore, for Thatcher to encourage clubs to build better facilities. I do believe that poor facilities were a contributory factor to the rise of football hooliganism, and was a reason why a lot of fans stayed away from attending. It certainly was not a game geared for the family in 1980's Britain. The way fans were treated was abysmal, absolutely shocking and diabolical. If you travelled by train you were often confronted by the massed ranks of the local police force or 'Thatcher's Thugs,' before being frog marched to your caged pens where you had to stand there for hours on end, sometimes in appalling weather conditions. It was like a war of attrition. There was no freedom of movement whatsoever. It was like that you did not live in a democracy but a vicious police state. The only way you could avoid this was if you arrived very early on your travels, not wearing any colours. Then you could sample the local hostelries. Some police forces were worse than others in their treatment, the most notorious being the Nottinghamshire force and West Midlands Police. More on them later.

When you are younger you often do things that you regret later on in life. I can very much relate to that in my own personal life. I can openly admit that I drunk far too much in my younger days, which had a profound effect on my behaviour. I suppose you could say that I got dragged into football hooliganism, although on a small scale. I was arrested and convicted a number of times over a four year period between 1981 – 1985. The first incident was when I returned from an away match at West Brom. It happened on Smethwick Rolfe Street railway station, the nearest one to the Hawthorns ground. It was a minor incident – urinating in a public place. A police officer caught me having a leak and I received an on the spot fine. The same thing happened again about 12 months later, one Saturday night in Blackburn town centre. I had returned from a home game and decided to have a few beers in Blackburn, so I got off the train there. I was well and truly out of itwhen I urinated on the wheel of a police car. I know what you are saying but it seemed to be the right thing to do at the time!!! Another on the spot fine. In 1983, I went to an away game at Coventry. I think I can recall it was the time when we got trounced 4 – 0, one of our worst performances during that period. I was sat in a stand that had Liverpool and Coventry fans. After Coventry scored their first goal, I jumped to my feet, being the worse for drink and gestured to the Coventry fans. I remember my exact words, "Come on you Coventry bastards have a f****** go."

I was arrested, spent several hours in a police cell and was bailed to appear in court. I had to return to Coventry several months later. I was charged and convicted of using threatening words and behaviour and breach of the peace. I had let my family, my very supportive parents down over these incidents, but it was not about to get any better.

In 1984, following another Liverpool home game, I was arrested on Preston railway station for smashing a lightbulb on the Ormskirk – Preston service. The British Transport Police took me in. I appeared in court in March 1985, which was to be my last court appearance. I was charged and convicted of criminal damage, and the magistrates had considered a custodial sentence. That was my wake up call. I have never appeared in court since.

Around the early 1980's, I met the Lancashire Reds, who travelled to games by train. We came from all over Lancashire – Burnley, Blackburn, Preston, Lancaster, Blackpool, Kirkham, Fleetwood, Lytham. I can remember some of their names even now – Ginger, Jeff, Audra, Mark, Toddy, Pete, Daz, Marsy, Wilksy, Peaky, Ronnie, Wurzel and Paula.

By 1986, a number of them had been sent down for a violent assault on a passenger on the London Underground. I was pretty stupid back then it must be said. I could have so easily have been with them that day. I have deliberately kept the names of those involved out of this, as I feel it would be unfair to penalise them in any way.

It was the game at Chelsea on the last day of the league season when we clinched the championship, and the first part of the double. I had to make a choice – see the title being clinched at Stamford Bridge or go to the FA Cup Final. Money was tight, so I chose the cup final. The Lancashire Crew, or at least several of them, never saw that cup final. What happened on the London Underground was nothing short of horrific and cowardly. They had gone down early, overnight, drinking in The Market Tavern, near London Bridge tube station, which opened up for market traders at 6am. After several hours drinking, they boarded the underground and on a station, the ringleader of the group, viciously, and without provocation, smashed a glass bottle into the skull of an innocent passer by. The others that were with him that day – stood idly by and did nothing to prevent the attack. I could have so easily been with them that day and my life would have taken a completely different turn. The fact that I hung around with this group and travelled to matches with them does, to a certain extent, sicken me with horror these days. Yet, that was my own choice, I cannot blame them for that, and at that time they were good mates. I am not trying to moralise or anything like that, I guess you could say that I'm a lot more sensible now and it is perfectly true to say that you do learn from your mistakes. I was a nasty piece of goods back then no question.

So what happened to the gang of thugs I hear you cry? I know for a fact that two of them got about 15 – 18 months each in a young offenders institution, for not preventing the attack even though they didn't actually take any part in the vicious assault. I know, talking to the youngest member of the crew, a few weeks afterwards, that he got off due to it being a first offence, and being younger than the others. As regards the ringleader, that is a different matter. He received at least three years for grievous and actual bodily harm coupled with the fact that when the police searched his house on information received, they found a stolen British Rail ticket machine. He had for well over a year printed off tickets for travel to matches for a £1 a go. What a bargain, for those going to the likes of Norwich and Souhampton for a quid!!! I was questioned, along with my girlfriend at the time, about purchasing such tickets. Obviously, we denied it. Later we found out that the police could not pin anything on us. After he was released from prison, I saw very little of the ringleader, and the others squarely put the blame on him. He ruined a lot of peoples lives of that there is no doubt, including his own. He was the eldest of that gang, and the others had a future. I know that one young lad had plans to go to university, and when he was released he told me he still hoped to go. As for the others, I saw the youngest lad regularly at games and we used to drink in The Sportsman before and after games. I saw another a few times too, where he told me a few fantasy tales of life inside, how 'I ran the wing, I was the Daddy' and all that old bull. But times move on, as do people.

In ending this chapter, I want to go back to the 29th of May 1985 and Heysel. Surely, another European Cup Final win was on the cards. What was to happen that day brought much horror and indeed some degree of shame on our great club. There is without doubt, a great deal of blame to be attached to some Liverpool fans that were there that fateful night in Brussels 27 years ago. Yet, there were other contributory factors at play too. I did not attend that final, as money was virtually non-existent at that time. We were at the height of Thatcherism and mass unemployment. I watched the events unfold on the TV. What I saw filled me with horror. I saw pictures of fans charging across a terrace. I saw much panic and distress. I saw a crumbling wall. I saw fear. Why? Why did this have to happen? Why did 39 innocent people have to die at the hands of yobs? This had never happened to us before in Europe. We had enjoyed a previously excellent record of behaviour, even with hooliganism being so rife. What caused the Red Army to 'change it's colours?'

The year previously we had played another European Cup Final in Rome, the scene of our first triumph seven years earlier. This was to be a different scenario, but with the same result. We were to play Roma on their home ground, hardly a neutral venue. The club argued the fact with UEFA, but as is the norm, it fell on deaf ears. So we had to travel to the cauldron that was The Stadio Olimpico and face Roma. Naturally, they had massive support, we were given around 15,000 tickets. A decent following, but not the 30,000 that were there seven years earlier. What happened that day was shocking, with knife attacks, stonings, beatings and the like. A nasty atmosphere that lived long in the memory of Liverpool fans. There were stories of how fans were lucky to get out of there alive. Yes, the European Cup was won for the fourth time, but not without bloodshed and violence. It set a tone for the final twelve months later when Liverpool met another Italian side, Juventus, to defend their crown. In the minds of some Liverpool supporters it was the perfect opportunity to extract some revenge for what happened at the hands of Roma fans. I would say that it was not logical thinking, as Juventus fans were not responsible for what happened in Rome. Yet some fans saw them as Italian and that Italians had caused the violence, so revenge was on the cards.

In 1985, we were at the height of football hooliganism, a mountainous peak of sadistic, horrific, bloody violence. Every club in the land had some kind of hooligan firm, and Liverpool were no different. There was a nasty minority to our support – the so-called 'Barmy Anny Road Army.' I would not say we were the worst, with the most nortoriety, far from it, but we had a nasty edge, especially in games against Manchester United, our bitterest and most hated rivals. It always seemed to kick off, if you pardon the footballing anallergy, both home and away. One of the most violent confrontations took place at the FA Cup semi-final at Goodison

Park. I saw it at first hand, with golf balls with sharp nails and screws inserted in them, used as a weapon to inflict as much pain as possible. A nasty, violent situation ensued. This was a few short weeks before the European Cup Final in Brussels. I do believe that that nasty element intended to travel to Belgium and inflict as much pain on the Italians as they had done on the Mancs. A lot of angry young men, with no job, no hope and no prospects under Thatcher. A time of rebellion. A time of 'screw you and screw your government and your policies. I want to be noticed.'

It was also a time, all over the country, of nasty racism with The National Front and Combat 18, a far-right group renowned for football violence and racial hatred. They saw Heysel as a boiling inferno waiting to explode, and they were going to trigger the time bomb and set the explosion. A perfect opportunity for racist scum from cockney clubs like Chelsea, Millwall and West Ham, to set something in motion and blame it all on Scousers. This so-called 'ultra-socialist, violent, jobless, crime-filled city' that Thatcher and others despised. To be honest it worked.

Heysel Stadium, in Brussels, was so inadequately unsuitable to hold the biggest match in European club football. It was an old, crumbling, antiquated ground, with chicken wire fencing supposed to segregate opposing fans, old barriers and even older stone walls. There were concerns made by both Liverpool and Juventus regarding the unsuitability of the ground as a European Cup Final venue. Again, it all fell on deaf ears. So UEFA must share some of the responsibility of what happened at Heysel. Another issue was why a section of terracing was given over to neutral Belgian fans. Liverpool's Chief Executive warned that these tickets could be snapped up by touts and sold on to Italian fans. This is exactly what happened. So in the large terrace behind the goal, which was split into three sections – X, Y and Z – Liverpool were given sections X and Y, whereas the so-called 'neutrals' were given section Z. The tension grew inside that terrace, missiles and abuse was hurled between

Liverpool and Juventus fans over a limp chicken wire fence. The police did little or nothing to react. The nastiness of Liverpool v Manchester United a few weeks earlier had transferred itself to Brussels and Liverpool v Juventus. The hotheaded hooligans of both clubs were fired up for a violent confrontation, which led to 39 deaths. The Liverpool fans, stoked up with hatred for Italians, following the violent and unprovoked attacks on them 12 months earlier, and a sheer, bloody lust for revenge, coupled with the egging on of racist thugs, connected to clubs with affiliations to Combat 18 and the National Front, charged the chicken wire fence to get at the Juventus fans. At the other end of the ground, Juventus fans, with scarves covering their faces, some brandishing knives, sticks and even pistols, were also ready for violent action. I saw all of this unfold on TV before my very eyes. I so easily could have been part of that, albeit as an innocent bystander. I also could have been sucked into the violence. One of the Lancashire Crew got sucked in, or so he said as much, when I saw him the following season. What many people do not know, if that Juventus fans started the missile throwing, and Liverpool fans reacted – badly. I am not making excuses for Liverpool fans, but merely stating facts.

Yes, as Liverpool fans, we must hold up our hands to take a fair share of the responsibility and blame for Heysel. After all, if we had not rushed the chicken wire fence, people would not have died. Yet, Juventus fans did not exactly cover themselves with a blaze of glory that night either. In fact, as I have just stated above, it was the Juventus who actually started the provoking and the throwing of missiles. They were spoiling for a fight, both in that terrace and at the other end of the ground. Some of them actually had guns for goodness sakes. The police were weak and ineffective. The ground was totally unsuitable and falling apart. The Belgian FA with their ticketing arrangements that were a complete shambles, and the ignorance of UEFA. The racist thugs whose sole purpose was to cause trouble and deflect the blame onto Liverpool fans. It is an absolute known fact that leaflets were being handed out by The National Front that night and the then Liverpool chairman, Sir John Smith, had evidence to prove it. Yes, Liverpool fans, who had their excellent reputation not only tarnished, but destroyed overnight, must hold up their hands to say sorry. We have said sorry, many times. Others should have too. Of those that were arrested 60% were Scousers, but 40% were not. I wonder how many were actual Liverpool fans, and how many were racist thugs from other clubs. I guess we will never know.

What gets me, and really does annoy me, is the notion and the falsehood that 'Heysel was all down to Scousers.' It simply, truthfully, was not. We get this whenever we play Manchester United from their so-called 'whiter than white' fans. Yet, today, in the modern era, more people are arrested at Old Trafford than at any other football ground in the country. We get the taunts of 'three European Cups without killing anybody.' Or 'justice for the 39.' Evidence, if any were needed, that Manchester United 'fans' have the least knowledge of any supporters in world football. First of all, four European Cup wins without any hint of trouble from Liverpool fans, and one final where the powder keg was lit, many deaths, and many causes. Another European Cup triumph in 2005, in Istanbul, with not one report of any trouble, nor one arrest.

Then we get the 'murderers' chants from the Mancs, and from Everton, even Chelsea. Do not get we started on that tiny West London club. If these people actually tried to look at the 'facts' and the definition of 'MURDER' then they would see that such a definition clearly states:

'MURDER - THE TAKING OF HUMAN LIFE IN A PRE-MEDITATED ACT'

Heysel was neither pre-meditated, nor was it murder. Then we come to the 'justice for the 39' calls. If you look at the evidence and the undeniable facts, 14 Liverpool fans were tried and convicted of involuntary manslaughter in the wake of the Heysel tragedy. Furthermore, the chief police officer in charge was also tried and convicted and was sent to prison for several months. So, there was 'JUSTICE FOR THE 39.'

Heysel was a disaster that shocked the world, and in which 39 people lost their lives. My heart goes out to them and their families, as does my thoughts and my prayers. Rest in Peace the Heysel 39. You'll Never Walk Alone. AMICZI – FRIENDSHIP.

Chapter Three

The Darkest Day:
The Hillsborough Disaster
Saturday the 15th of April 1989

1. My Story

The very first thing I can recall about the 15th of April 1989, and I remember it vividly to this very day, as though it was only yesterday, was what a beautifully warm, sunny spring morning it was. The sun shone brightly, a brilliantly radiant blue sky, a few puffy white clouds that soon disappeared, and birds singing majestically in the blossoming trees. It was as if everything was perfect that day. A day to be happy and at peace. But, as we know, that peace was a temporary one, which would be shattered in the worst day in British sporting history.

I woke up with an excited buzz. I was off to the FA Cup semi-final and a return to Hillsborough, just like last year. A close game, which Liverpool won 2 – 1 with a John Aldridge double. It was the same opponents as well – Nottingham Forest. I recalled what a good day out it had been. I had travelled up by train from Burnley, got to the ground early and had a few bevies. There was a good banter, the Sheffield folks had welcomed us into their city and there was no crowd trouble. The police were friendly enough and had everything sussed out. They had channelled fans into Leppings Lane through barriers once you had shown an officer your ticket. All very sensible, all very relaxed. I sat on a wall by the river which ran along Leppings Lane, before entering the ground. It was about two thirty. The obvious, direct route was down the tunnel to the central pens, but it had been closed off. We had to choose another option, so I went into a side pen. I think I can recall it being Pen 1, by the police control box. It was absolutely chocker block, a bit uncomfortable really. But no worries, I had stood like this for years watching football, I could cope. I thought the same again this year please, with the same result. Not a problem.

I got dressed and wore my red Liverpool home shirt with a blue sweatshirt cum jumper over the top, which had a collar and three brown buttons and a large LFC crest emblazoned on it. I had on jeans and trainers and took my red cap and scarf with me too. I was going by car this year, with friends (or they were at that time). There was the driver, Edward, and the two girls, Sharon and Lynn. They all had seat tickets for the North Stand, I had a Leppings Lane terrace ticket. We enjoyed the sunshine and had a good laugh as we journeyed across the Pennines to Sheffield. There were some delays on the motorway and on the outskirts, the police were stopping and searching mini buses and coaches. A bit over sensitive I thought. This was early, before midday. We got there early for a good parking spot, which was on a large pub car park, by the Travellers pub, with the Gate Inn next door. A few fans were milling around, and we opted for the craic of the pub. I cannot recall which pub we went to – the Travellers or the Gate. The others stayed for about an hour before deciding to walk up to the ground. The pub filled up and Liverpool fans sang their vast array of songs and had good banter with the locals it was all very friendly, just like at every football match at every ground up and down the country, where fans mingle and go for a few drinks. It was all lively, but with no drunkenness or any nastiness attached to it. I had a bite to eat and a few pints, nothing too excessive – everybody was perfectly happy. We even bought raffle tickets for a local charity. I headed for the ground at about two fifteen or two twenty. I thought it would be nice and civilised just like last year. What I found was it became very busy, and the police were irate. It was the total opposite to 1988. There was an awful, raw tension there. It was very striking. There was pushing and jostling as people tried to find freedom of movement, but it remained good natured, amongst the fans that is. There were no barriers, no ticket checking, no channelling. You were left to your own devices. You were on your own. What we have heard over the years, from lies and fabrications regarding Hillsborough, has been the verbal assault and blame on Liverpool fans. Of drunken, ticketless yobs, of a nasty crowd intent on getting inside the ground at any cost, of abusive violent thugs. The real truth of the matter is that what I saw is totally different. A statement of truth, and not lies. The lies are reserved for South Yorkshire Police, Kelvin Mackenzie and others. There was a massive crowd build up, yes that is very true. But that had to do with a combination of poor policing, over sensitive police powers in their stop and search policy, making fans late, as well as roadwork's and hold ups on the motorway. Not drunkenness. Yes, some fans went for a few drinks, but, as I have already stated, so do many fans up and down the country at every ground and at every match. This is hardly unusual.

As I walked down Leppings Lane and the pace slowed, that bottleneck became tighter and the further I got down there the more distressing and uncomfortable it became. Where was all this so-called drunken thuggery then? I saw a few lads sat on a garden wall drinking cans of lager, and singing songs, being a bit boisterous, and one teenage lad having a leak in the same garden – silly behaviour yes, but drunken behaviour? I don't think so. As far as I am concerned, and with what I witnessed, there were no drunken yobs on view that day. No 'tanked up mob' as was suggested by Bernard Ingham, Margaret Thatcher's Press Secretary. Another absolute and blatant lie.

The walk was becoming increasingly slow towards the Leppings Lane turnstiles, almost to a stop, as more and more fans walked towards those gates. It seemed to take for ages. The nearer you got, the more you heard the calls of distress, of pain and of fear. There was some anger directed to the police, but this was due to the fact that fans were becoming increasingly concerned and that people were going to get hurt, or worse. I too, became increasingly concerned for my own safety. It was now developing into a crush on that street, as the bottleneck tightened it's grip on the huge swell of humanity. A number of fans tried to get out of the way by climbing onto the wall by the river, others climbed to the top of turnstiles not to gain entry without a ticket but to escape the crush around them. The calls then became screams, with people in real pain. It was very plain to see that many people were in deep distress and some were getting hurt. A police horse bolted, knocking fans out of the way. Yet, the police still did nothing.

"There are people getting hurt," I heard one fan say.

"Someone is going to die," I heard another one scream.

"You have to do something." was a further cry. Yet, absolutely nothing was done.

I was penned in by the turnstile wall with no freedom of movement, no chance of escape. I sweated heavily, almost breathlessly. I honestly feared for my own safety. There was a shakiness to my body, a real abject fear. A frighteningly dangerous situation had developed, and I was right in the centre of it. I was in real danger of being crushed against that wall. I was virtually right next to the gate as the senior officer called out to the police control room via his radio.......

"You need to open the gate........Open the gate."

He was very frantic in his call. After what seemed like hours but in reality, was only a matter of minutes, the large concertina blue gate (Gate C) was unlocked and the distressed fans, in blessed relief, flooded into the ground. I was one of them. At last I could breathe and calm down. A blessed relief. When we got in there, there were no police officers or stewards to guide us, as fan after fan pulled out their match tickets. Where were these 'ticketless fans' then? The natural reaction was to head straight for the dark tunnel for the central pens of 3 and 4. I did not recall the previous year when I headed for the side pens. After all, in 1988, the tunnel was closed off with the pens full. Everybody assumed that there was space in the central pens so we headed there to get a better spec. Unknown to us, however, those pens were already full.

As I entered the tunnel everything seemed so dark, so unreal, so eerie. There was a deep, dark, frightening reality to it all. There was little or no light, just one light bulb as I recall. It was a steep gradient of 1 in 6 to the top of the pens, but the darkness made you stutter and lose your footing somewhat, during that drop down. There was an even deeper fear engulfing me now. So many fans poured into that tunnel it was impossible to breathe in such small a space. It was impossible to move or turn back, you were just pushed further inside by the mass swell behind you and by your side. A number fell to the floor, probably to their deaths, unknowingly trampled upon by fellow Liverpool supporters. There was no air inside that tunnel. Absolutely none. The fact that it was a very warm April day made that even more evident. What seemed like another endless age, concluded when I finally reached some kind of daylight and the fullness of those cramped central pens hit you square in the face. Another deep fear engulfed me. There was absolutely no room, whatsoever. Nothing. I could not move one inch, my hands and arms imprisoned with the rest of those fans in there.

As I stood at the top of that terrace by a fence that separated Pens 3 & 4, I had to decide which way to go. To the left was Pen 3, to the right Pen 4. I chose right. All these years, I thought I had been in Pen 3, but in reality it was Pen 4. I found this to be the case after viewing film footage of the disaster and actually spotting myself near the fence that separated the two central pens, just inside Pen 4 and near the top. So, I apologise to everyone for that. I was near the fence that ran down the terrace, at the top. I felt a surge from the back. But it was not like a normal surge that happened when I stood on The Kop at Anfield, this was different. This was real pain, as other fans were pushed against me. I was slowly being crushed from behind, my back aching in deep intensity and without any kind of relief. The vice tightened even more, life being squeezed out of people, life being squeezed out of me. By this point the game had started, and I distinctly remember Peter Beardsley hitting the bar. Another massive surge came, even bigger than the previous one. I was crushed violently against a barrier, my chest full of deep pain, and sharp surges continuously shot up my back. My whole life flashed before me, as if I was about to lose that life. I screamed in deep, painful agony, just managing to relieve the pressure by pushing backwards slightly to gain a small, almost insignificant space, a mere inch or two. I was breathless, but not really realising how actually close to death I had been. Not long after, the game was abandoned. I was being pushed further from behind, and there was a body beneath my feet. I stumbled, breathlessly, and was about to drop to the floor as my knees, gave way, my legs feeling like jelly, buckled beneath me. Luckily, I was pulled up by a fellow fan. I remember his very words to this day:

"You're not going to die, not today."

In fact, I have remembered those words each and every day for 23 years. Indeed, at times, those words have haunted me, even frightened me. Yet, that guy saved my life. A guardian angel in Red looking after me. When I looked round in the mass swell he was gone. That has haunted me to this day, I only hope he got out of there alive. I have always wished I could have met him and been able to thank him for what he did for me. I have thought deeply about that for 23 years.

I still had not got out of that horrific pen. The crush was intensifying if anything. That tightening vice was crushing every ounce of life out of many brave Reds, which was becoming even more evident. I was flung violently into that barrier once again, my chest expanding, crushed from behind intensely for what seemed like forever, but in reality was about less than a minute   Another violent, sharp pain just shot up my back, and I felt breathless, helpless, a deep faintness came across my forehead, my life flashing before me.   I was going under, no mistake.   I screamed once more, in absolute unbearable pain and just about managed to gain enough space, slightly more than the previous time, behind me, to relieve the intense pressure on my back and on my chest.   A number of fans were being pulled up into the stand above, and gradually, slowly but surely, a little space appeared and I could breathe, just a little.   I could not breathe fresh air as I clutched my painful chest.   If that small but significant space had not developed at that precise moment I would have gone under into unconsciousness and probably death.   I was being asphyxiated at that moment of that there is no doubt.

There was a vile smell there that afternoon. An awful, uncompromising smell.   The nasty smell of death.   It was an awful smell, and something which you never expect to breathe in through your nostrils.   I stepped over bodies as I followed other fans in the slow process out onto the pitch, but I was just in a complete daze.   I dared not look down on those that had perished.   Everything seemed so unreal. Yet it was real, this was happening, and it was happening to me.   It is something that would change my life forever.   I had witnessed death, much death, and had fought to save my own life.   I could not see much in front of me as I had lost my glasses in that pen.   I just wandered around that pitch in a mind blowing, life altering, numb shock, in tears, and in pain.   This just did not seem like reality to me.   I did see a number of bodies laid down on the pitch, every ounce of life squeezed out of them in such a horrific, violent way.   One was a young boy, his face a purple blue, a few specks of blood, eyes glazed, mouth open, a painful look.   I am pretty sure it was the youngest victim, Jon-Paul Gilhooley.   A few seconds later, his face was covered.   I saw fans use advertising hoardings as makeshift stretchers, trying to save lives, as they ferried the injured and dying to safety. I saw one ambulance, just one. There were many fans injured and dying and one f****** ambulance. The indisputable fact that there were 44 ambulances laying idle outside the stadium, whilst people lay dying is an absolute disgrace. The fact that ambulance drivers and paramedics were told by police officers that 'you cannot go on the pitch, they are still fighting.' Yes, people were fighting – fighting to save their own lives, and the lives of others. Absolute disgusting and unforgivable. What chance did they have? I saw many brave fans act as rescuers and comforters. Was this the work of a drunken mob? Or violent, ticketless fans? No. It was the work of selfless heroes doing the job of the emergency services. The emergency services that failed the fans, who lay dying and injured that fateful April day.

I had lost it completely. I just wandered around that pitch in a blind panic, clutching my chest, gasping for air, feeling my back. There were others doing the same as me so I wasn't alone. A number of fans asked me if I was alright, if I needed help.

"Are you alright, mate?"

"Can I help you?"

"Are you injured?"

I just shook my head.

"I want my friends. I need to find my friends," I sobbed.

I was no use whatsoever. I still feel deep guilt about that to this very day. I continued to wander aimlessly around that pitch. As fans rescued other fans, as fans desperately tried to save lives, as fans used advertising boards as makeshift stretchers, I wandered uncontrollably in tears, shaking my an autumn leaf, around that pitch. I just could not force myself to do anything else.

I cannot recall how long I was on that pitch for. All that I can say is that I could not find my friends, who were sat in the North Stand, no matter how hard I looked. I returned to the pen and asked a policeman if I could search for my glasses. He agreed to my request. There was a pile of belongings in a heap at the bottom of that terrace, mainly scarves and caps, but clothes as well. I searched but I could not find my glasses. I picked up a cap, it looked like mine, but I wasn't absolutely sure. I honestly don't know if it was. I often think had I picked up a cap that belonged to one of the 96? Was it really my own cap? I was traumatised beyond belief and recognition. The original onset of my battle with the terrible psychological condition of PTSD – or Post Traumatic Stress Disorder. My life changed forever. As I stood in that now empty pen, I could still smell that horrible, sickening stench of death. There was no fresh air in there whatsoever. The still, warm day made it even more pungent, more sickening. The living nightmare of death, avoidable death. I looked at the mangled wreckage of the buckled barriers, the ripped open fencing, the killing fields of Hillsborough. I asked myself, WHY? As my mind wandered in a trance, someone approached me. It was someone who I knew through Edward, who went to Liverpool games sometimes. Looking back, I could not recall his name, not for a long time. But now, as I write this, I remember his name was Alan. I know that sounded awful, and pretty ignorant, but it just did not come back to me, not for a long time. He asked me how I was. I told him that I had been in the central pens, where so much death had occurred, and asked him if he was okay and where he had been stood. He told me he had been in one of the side pens and that he could not grasp what had happened. He wandered off in a total daze. I still stood there feeling helpless and all alone. A policeman told me that I had to leave the pen and I headed for the tunnel. He stopped me and said that the tunnel had been sealed off. I thought about that and said to myself, "Like it should have been well before kick off." I couldn't talk. Everything was just too emotional for me. I was in a dazed kind of hell that I just could not escape from.

I had to somehow grasp some kind of reality, as this all seemed so unreal to me, even though it was real. All too real. I had to focus, and what flashed across my mind was the fact that I had to contact my family back home – my Mum and Dad, and my brother, Anthony. They told me later that they watched all the horrors of the disaster unfold before their very eyes on Grandstand. They kept helplessly looking to see if they could spot me on the pitch during the TV coverage. They continuously rang the emergency numbers, without success. What they felt, what many other families felt, watching it all unfold on national television must have been mind numbingly awful. Not knowing what had happened to their loved ones, if they were alive or dead, waiting for a reassuring phone call, or worse news to tell you that your loved one had died.

I walked back onto the pitch and exited the ground by another route, by the side of the South Stand. I walked back up Leppings Lane, still occasionally looking back towards Gate C, in total, utter disbelief in what I had witnessed. There was an eerie silence now on that street, not the noisy, bustling jostle there had been a couple of hours before. No screams of panic, no shouts for help. I saw grown men sat on the floor in a heap crying their eyes out. This had been the absolute worst day of my entire life. My darkest day, the darkest hours of unimaginable hell. I know that it is a blindingly obvious statement, but to witness death, in this case multiple death, is just the worst thing that you could ever encounter. Furthermore, you never, ever get over it. I looked for a telephone box to ring home. What few there were had seemingly endless lines of fans queued up impatiently, frantically, wanting to do the same thing. It was impossible. I decided to walk back to the car, slowly, still looking back, tears rolling down my face. I was still in deep, physical pain, trying to hide it as much as I could. The others were not there when I arrived. Obviously they were looking for me. What exactly were they feeling? I just pushed my head down onto the roof of the car and closed my eyes. I heard other fans scream in emotional pain, some punching or kicking car doors. I waited for what seemed like ages. In reality it was several minutes. At first there was a total, eerie silence, before they spoke. I was in total traumatic shock that I couldn't speak. They said things like:

"My God, are you alright?"

"Is that blood?" (I held the cap to my side so it looked like blood)

"No, it's my cap," I muttered nervously.

"We looked for you but we couldn't find you."

I responded emotionally, the words struggling to come out.

"I tried to find you. I looked in the stands, but couldn't see much, I lost my glasses. I was wandering around that pitch for ages."

Now I was shaking uncontrollably, like a leaf being hit with a huge gust of wind. I could hardly cope with the enormity of what had happened to me, and to many others. It was like I had been knocked to the floor and couldn't get back up.

We headed up to Wadsley Bridge, a steep uphill climb at the top of the main road. I cannot remember if we walked or drove up. I think we walked. We were desperate to find a telephone to contact our families. A lot of other fans were doing the same. At the top of the hill we talked to a group of young lads who were desperately trying to find one of their friends. He was missing and they were frantic with worry. I remember the words of one of those lads to this very day:

"He's only seventeen."

I have often wondered if he was one of the 96.

What I can recall about that afternoon, and it is something which really touched me, and many other Liverpool supporters, was the limitless generosity of the Sheffield people in that locality. We hear, even now, that a lot of the Sheffield public, or certainly a fair percentage, as much as high as 50% still blame Liverpool fans for the disaster. It certainly was not the case that afternoon. A lot of the local residents had wandered down to Wadsley Bridge to see what was happening, and to offer their support. There is a council estate close to Wadsley Bridge, and a lot of Liverpool fans headed for there, invited into the homes of the locals, to ring home and to be offered cups of tea, food and much needed comfort, sympathy and understanding. This was offered to us by an elderly couple. They were absolutely wonderful to us, and it is something which I will never, ever forget. They took us into their home, a council flat on the first floor and asked if we wanted anything to eat. We politely declined. I don't think anyone who had been there that day and witnessed what confronted us that April afternoon could possibly eat a thing. We decided to have very sweet tea, which apparently, is good for you when suffering from deep shock. This lovely couple offered much needed support and told us what had unfolded on TV. They were there for us when we needed them, something which was greatly appreciated. After we had drunk the sweet tea, they asked us if we would like to ring home. Obviously, we jumped at the chance. I was the only one with a terrace ticket, so you would have thought that I would be the first to use the telephone, but no not a chance. I was in too much turmoil to argue with Lynn who rang first. I always found her to be at times, somewhat childish, even selfish. The others were to blame too. After all, everyone knew in their families that they had seat tickets so would not have been in the crush. I was the only one who could have been injured or worse. I was injured. Maybe you think that I'm being over-sensitive, but I feel that I should have been given the first opportunity to contact my family. Eventually, I could ring home. I was shaking like a leaf. I was stressed out to the max, in total, deep shock. I was struggling to hold back the tears. I was still shaking uncontrollably. I dialled the number. As soon as it rang my Mum picked up the telephone. There was fear and nervousness in her voice. Obviously thinking it was the dreaded call 'you need to come to Sheffield.'

"Hello" she said in deep trepidation.

"It's me Mum. Oh it was horrible…"

That was it I lost it completely. I wept openly without restraint. It takes a lot for me to cry. This was a lot.

"Don't cry," protested Lynn.

How could she tell me not to cry, I thought. She didn't have to fight for her life. She wasn't injured. She hadn't been crushed inside that horrific pen. Maybe I was being harsh. Maybe she was trying to comfort me in some way. Maybe she wanted me to stay strong. I reacted angrily, or as angry as I could.

"If I want to cry, I'll cry."

I focused back on the telephone conversation with my Mum.

"I alright Mum, I'm safe."

I didn't tell her there and then about my injuries, just that we were in a Sheffield couple's home, and that we would soon be on our way back to Burnley. The others insisted that I got treatment for my injuries, but I told them I wanted to go home first and that I would get checked out at the hospital in Burnley. No way was I going to be treated in Sheffield. As we left, Sharon got the telephone number and the address of the couple. We thanked them for all that they had done for us and said our goodbyes.

The journey home was just the most awful journey that you could make. I was glad that I was not driving. I don't think that I could have got us home the state I was in. I was fearful, angry, frustrated, tearful, anxious. A powerful box, full of different emotions. I thought we were going to crash, that's how bad I was. The deep anxiety was setting in. I remained totally and utterly silent. Not a word came from my lips, at least until I heard THAT lie. The car radio was on. The death toll kept on rising – 30, 40, 50, 60. When you hear such things you are just speechless. You cannot take it all in, you are left feeling totally gobsmacked, unaware of your emotions or what to do with them.

"Oh my God," gasped Edward.

He was the driver. I must praise him, therefore, how he got us home. He was superb. I know he had a lot of faults, I guess we all do, but that evening he was just fantastic. Then the words were uttered by Graham Kelly, FA Secretary.

"It appears, according to the police, that Liverpool fans forced open the gate."

That was it for me. I just could not stay silent anymore. A deep anger and rage left my body through my mouth. It just had to be said.

"The f****** liar," I screamed. "The police opened that gate, I was f****** there. The f****** lying bastards."

The now infamous blatant Duckenfield lie. Nobody else in the car uttered one single word. I guess they knew what kind of state I was in.

The death toll rose even higher as I arrived home. The two girls were dropped off first. I arrived home not knowing where I was, or what to do. I was completely lost and still in a total daze. As I stepped over the doorstep I instantly became a different person. A part of me died that day, it totally took away part of my life forever.

There was news coverage, almost continuously on the TV. I now had to face that, too. Yet, it was strange. I had to watch it like I couldn't get enough of it, like I could maybe change the course of events. In reality, I couldn't but my mental state meant that I had to watch it and relive it all. It was there again, repeated – Duckenfield's blatant lie. I had to contact friends and extended family to tell them that I was okay. I went round to some friends of my parents who had been worried about my safety and told them everything, including the lies. I felt that I had to right this wrong. A very severe, and calculated wrong.

I went to the hospital, which was only a short walk. My body ached, my chest hurt, and my back and stomach were in deep pain. I arrived in Casualty and waited. I was finally called in to see a doctor. He was German, from Hamburg. He kept going on about Kevin Keegan and Liverpool. I normally would have engaged him in conversation, but it just was not registering. He had a look at me. When I removed my shirt my whole chest and stomach was covered in bruises. I was in deep pain. He asked me to cough. When I tried it was a breathlessly excruitiating pain. I was sent for an x-ray. I had ECG tests. My heart was fine.

The x-ray revealed badly bruised and cracked ribs, some chest damage and signs of crush asphyxia – that is how close I was to death. I was given medication for pain relief. The doctor advised me that I could have problems in later years following the injuries. I have chest problems to this day, which flares up from time to time and it is honestly quite frightening when I have those episodes. I also have aching back issues. The worst for me though, has been the psychological problems. I have suffered from PTSD or Post Traumatic Stress Disorder from that day. I have had to face the nightmares, the anxiety, the fear, the panic attacks, the flashbacks, waking up in a cold sweat, low self esteem, total lack of confidence, anger, frustration and paranoia. It is just a terrible illness that I would not wish on anybody.

I did not sleep a wink that night. I just relived it all, over and over again. I cried constantly. I dared not go to sleep, as I feared that I was about to die. It all seemed so unreal. I could not eat and I was in constant pain. The worst day of my life, followed by the absolute worst night.

2. A Survivor's Story

I first met this unnamed survivor on Facebook. We were both in those central pens of Leppings Lane, and have suffered similarly with PTSD ever since. This is his version of events of the 15th of April 1989, in his own words:

"It was a sunny April day when we travelled to Sheffield to watch the Reds. I met my mates – had what I needed my ciggies, match ticket and a couple of cans. We drove to Sheffield in a van and had a good laugh, sang songs, a game of cards and the like. As we neared Sheffield, the police had set up roadblocks to search vehicles. We were waved through, but the police had an arrogant look about them that day. Anyway, we parked up at about 1:40pm, so we were there in plenty of time. I joined a queue for a bevy in the pub, and had a couple of pints. The walk to the ground was down this long hill. As I got to the turnstiles things just didn't seem right, there were too many people there on that tight street. A crush built up. I was eventually pinned up against the large blue gate, grabbing hold of one of my mates, to feel secure I guess. The panic there was huge, rising all the time. I heard the senior officer plead for that gate to be opened. Eventually it was and we headed straight down the tunnel, with my ticket still in my hand. I went right into Pen 3. I had lost all but one of my mates, just me and Kenny. We got to the front but couldn't see much at all, so we attempted to push our way back to get a better view. It's a good job we did looking back. It was too tight in there, in fact it was frightening.

Kenny lost his glasses as the crush got worse. I honestly couldn't breathe. I started thinking of loved ones, of my Dad. It was so tight in there, I received an arm in my throat and I saw people turning blue. I heard Kenny say that he was 'going' and the next moment his head went to one side. The anger inside of me rose up as my mate, Kenny, was dying next to me. I started to headbutt him, in sheer desperation, to

34

bring him back. I did this time after time, up to ten I think. In the end, Kenny came back. I had unknowingly fractured his cheekbone. There was a young lad in front of me on the floor. He had sticky out ears. I reached out and grabbed him, holding him in one hand, my mate Kenny in the other. Then another surge came and I thought my end was nigh. I felt like I was floating, then I came down to the floor, but still holding on to Kenny and the young lad. I gladly realised that I was still alive. I tried to ask others to help me get this young lad off his knees. There was this one bloke who I asked, but he was dead on his feet. Another surge came, this time it was impossible to hang on. The next thing I knew, the young lad had left my hand, he was gone. The barrier creaked under all the pressure, before it twisted and snapped. That was it, we all fell over to the floor. I actually thought my legs had broken, but that feeling of choking had gone now.

My legs had not broken, I managed to get to my feet. The pile of bodies was high. Why? I thought why all this death? I saw Kenny and threw him over all the carnage. He managed to climb over the fence and get out onto the pitch. I started grabbing bodies and pulled them away. I sat there for a while, totally exhausted. I spotted this copper who was smiling – smiling at a time like this. I climbed to my feet to try to find a way out. No luck. The exit gate was firmly locked. I clambered over into the next pen, falling. Some other lads caught me and pulled me back to my feet. I thank God for them. I had to find Kenny, that was my next thought. I went over the top and out onto the pitch. I saw him in the penalty box, lying there with pain in his eyes. We both cried our eyes out. I had to find my other mates. I walked around the pitch, seeing other fans vomiting. I heard a shout from the stand above, my mates were safe.

There were hundreds of fans walking around aimlessly. Then the Forest fans chanted and taunted, 'Get off the f****** pitch.' They just didn't have a clue what had gone on. But we were angry, it was boiling over. We charged towards that end wanting to kick those sick bastards.

After all, they seemed to be mocking those that had died. The police came from nowhere and formed a cordon with police dogs, just watching on as brave fans rescued the injured and the dying.

Kenny wanted to find his glasses, so he tried to drag me back onto that terrace. I left him to it, I just could not go back in there – all those shoes, the clothes, the twisted barrier. We somehow left the ground, how I just don't know. We walked up that big hill and I heard one guy shout 'pricks,' as he jumped on a car. We all got to the van and greeted each other. As I sat in the van everything sank in, the realisation of what happened. The awful stench of blood, sick and piss covered my clothes. I just wanted to get back home. We found a pub and rang home. It was a tearful conversation as I talked with my Mum and Dad. The journey home was just a complete blur. I just wanted to be back home in Liverpool with my family. I kept thinking about that young lad. When I got home I just hugged my parents. I had been so close to death.

I sat alone that night after I sent my Mum and Dad out to the pub. My head was in my hands. I watched 'Match of the Day' only it wasn't the usual programme quite obviously. It looked back at the horrific events of the day. They said that 90 had died. I just sat there crying. I could not get my head round it all, I kept thinking about that young lad. He was only a kid. I didn't sleep that night, a regular thing over the years.

On the Sunday I looked at the papers, reliving it all again. Those pictures haunt me to this very day. I went to the pub later on and Kenny was there. He thanked me for 'saving his life.' I didn't want thanks, I wanted someone to talk to, reassurance, a caring hug. I kept thinking about 'that lad.' Then came the LIES in The S*n and all the crap. 'We killed our own?' 'We robbed the dead?' 'Pissed on bodies?' 'Kicked and punched cops?' That is certainly not what I saw. I saw brave fans as heroes, whilst cops did F*** ALL. You know that you stood there laughing at us, whilst people died alone in that crush. You know you pushed them back off the fence, despite the pleas, despite the scenes of death. You know the ambulance came on the pitch, but you lied about it. This is the truth because I was there.'

Those are two very different, but in many ways, very similar stories of the experiences of two Liverpool fans at Hillsborough. Both the fellow survivor and I were in the central pens of Leppings Lane. We both survived in those pens when many others did not. We have both suffered from PTSD or Post Traumatic Stress Disorder and have struggled to cope for 23 years. We both had a ticket, as did all of the fans in there that day. We both witnessed the TRUTH and have had to put up with the vile lies and fabrications, and the deliberately planned and thought out cover ups for over two decades. Our experiences are just two examples that many fans have to tell of that day. These are written here as absolute proof of what happened at Hillsborough on the 15th of April 1989 so that the world knows what REALLY happened. It is perfectly clear and true in using the words of Anne Williams, in this one final statement – 'We have the truth, now we want JUSTICE.'

3. Anne's Story

Anne Williams is a remarkable lady. I first met Anne, through Facebook, where I joined her support group, HOPE FOR HILLSBOROUGH. Through internet and telephone conversations, we got to know each other, supported each other, and told each others story. Of course, I already knew about Anne Williams through her wonderful book, WHEN YOU WALK THROUGH THE STORM, which tells of the tragic loss of her son, Kevin, at Hillsborough, and of Anne's endless, continuing fight for justice. This is Anne's story:

"On that morning, Saturday the 15th of April, Kevin came into the newsagents shop where I worked for his crisps and cans of coke. Kevin was with his friend, Andy Duncan, and they went to Sheffield together on the special train. He had already made up his lunch box the night before – cheese butties and a kit kat. Kevin wore a beige sweatshirt, chinos and Reebok trainers. He also had a blue jacket tied around his waist. Kevin told me that he would be home by 9 o'clock. As he went to the door he shouted 'No worries Mum, 3 – 0.' That is the last time I saw my son alive.

I finished work at lunchtime, and had the radio on. I heard them say that the match had been stopped and there was trouble at Hillsborough. My husband, Steve, told me to switch the TV on. It looked like a pitch invasion, people seemed to be wandering around not knowing where they were going. I heard on the news that there were 25 dead. By the time I had got to the British Legion club, the death toll was up to 74. It was packed in there, everybody watching the coverage on the TV screen.

The telephone never stopped ringing. Each time it rang, I hoped and prayed that it was Kevin, but each time it was friends wanting to know if we had heard any news. We tried the emergency number constantly, but it was pointless, it was always engaged. Later on that evening, Andy Duncan's Dad rang to tell us that Andy had been injured and was being treated at the hospital in Southport – those that were injured but could physically walk were told to get treatment at their local hospital. Andy had told his Dad that he had lost Kevin in a huge surge. He had tried to go back to the pen to find Kevin but was marched off the ground by the police. We now knew that Kevin was involved in the crush.

The seemingly endless wait was just the worst kind of torture. I just could not wait anymore, I had to go to Sheffield and try to find Kevin. I cried all the way there. Eventually we got to the ground and were directed to a local school. We were seen by social workers, but still no sign of Kevin. We were then told to go to the Medico-Legal centre in Watery Street. I have never been so frightened as I was then. When we arrived there, there were people and police everywhere. We sat in a courtroom and waited. I heard screaming, I knew that they had found that someone had died. There was death all around us, it was in the air itself. A man in a white coat approached us and asked us if we would look at some Polaroid photos. He warned us that they might be distressing. All the photos were pinned to a board. There was just a mass of pictures, but all that I could see was Kevin. His face jumped out at me, he looked so peaceful. I was told by a social worker that they were getting Kevin ready so that I could identify him. Yet, I was so frightened. I was frightened of Kevin. I was frightened of his death. Another man in a white coat took me to a small room. There were velvet curtains, and the man in the white coat pulled a cord and the curtains opened. Kevin was behind a glass screen, so I couldn't touch him. Yet, I wanted to touch him. He looked asleep, except for one eye that was half open.

Before we went home, I was given a small plastic bag that contained Kevin's belongings – his train ticket, his match ticket, three £1 coins and his 'horn of life' and chain. I vowed that I would wear that around my neck forever.'

Chapter Four

The Body Belongs to the Coroner, Not You

When you lose a loved one in tragic circumstances, be it a son or daughter, father or mother, brother or sister, you would normally expect to receive support and understanding, not to mention a fair degree of sympathy and pastoral care from a number of agencies. This could be from the police, ambulance service, fire brigade, hospital staff such as doctors or nurses, social workers, the clergy and others. You would imagine such agencies, who are highly trained for such circumstances, would be more than willing to offer such services to you when you are in deep grief, and that they would have the sensitivity to offer some kind of care to the relatives of loved ones who have died. It should be especially so in major disasters. However, at Hillsborough, this was somewhat different, which makes this disaster almost unique.

If you are told, with crass insensitivity and without feeling that,

"THE BODY BELONGS TO THE CORONER, NOT YOU,"

How would you react? You would not believe it could possibly happen. Yet it did happen, and it happened in the immediate aftermath of the Hillsborough Disaster. The loved ones who lost members of their family that day, just wanted a few precious moments to say goodbye, to hold them dearly for one last time, to hold their hand and to weep for them. Why was this basic human right denied them? There is no clear explanation why this would happen, and there is no logic to it. The distraught families, many of whom travelled over the Pennines that night, or others who were at the match, were treated to a tirade of accusations, volatile questioning and aggressive interrogation, regarding the levels of alcohol their loved ones had consumed or whether or not they were in possession of a ticket. What did this have to do with the identification process? Imagine for a minute, if you were in the shoes of a bereaved member of your own family and you had lost someone at Hillsborough. How would you feel at this questioning? How would you react to the interrogation by officers from South Yorkshire Police? I know that I would be very, very angry. Despite all this, the bereaved kept their dignity that night. I am amazed that they managed to show so much self-restraint amid all this vile provacation, because I'm not sure that I could have done likewise.

Furthermore, when they came to the gymnasium, which was being used as a temporary mortuary at the back of the North Stand, to take part in the identification process, they were treated to a rushed, highly insensitive way of formal identification. Whether it was to look at pictures taken with Polaroid cameras of their loved ones, in deep pain, specks of blood of their faces or that anguished look of deathly blue, or to see the body bag unzipped and to quickly identify the body and then ushered away without a final chance to hold them, to say goodbye, whichever way you look at it there is no doubt that it smacked of vile, insensitive and degrading actions. To utter those words "THE BODY BELONGS TO THE CORONER, NOT YOU," is just the most utterly deplorable action you could possibly take.

So why was this action taken?

There was a plan of action in place. A deliberate, thought out plan of action to shift the blame onto Liverpool supporters. This all started with Duckenfield, the match commander for South Yorkshire Police, and his initial blatant lie that supporters had forced open the gate. If the true facts did get out then a lot of heads could roll. Were these the same Liverpool supporters who acted as brave rescuers? Were these the same Liverpool supporters who desperately tried to save lives? Were these the same Liverpool supporters who used makeshift stretchers and ferried the injured and dying to safety and who tried to give the kiss of life to their fellow dying fans? Were these the same Liverpool supporters who were exonerated of any wrong doing in The Taylor Report and were in fact praised by Lord Justice Taylor for their actions, whereas certain officers within the South Yorkshire force 'froze. ' This was hardly the actions of a drunken mob, or of ticketless thugs.

The decision to use the gymnasium as a temporary mortuary had been a collective one. Those involved included the Assistant Chief Constable, Chief Superintendent Addis, head of South Yorkshire CID, and of course Dr. Stefan Popper, the Sheffield Coroner. The gymnasium was partitioned off into three sections – at the far end was the temporary mortuary to house the bodies, which were fully clothed and placed in body bags and laid out on the gymnasium floor in rows. Each body was to be numbered and one police officer assigned to look after that body. A cloth or sponge was also given to wipe the face of the victim. Furthermore, each and every face was photographed using a Polaroid camera. The centre section was reserved for police officers to partake in refreshments, for them to 'enjoy' meals, if that's the right word, and have cups of tea or coffee. No mention of offering some kind of support to the bereaved families. The notion of 'looking after their own' immediately springs to mind. Yet, who in their right mind would want to eat when there were bodies on the gymnasium floor, of people who had died in such horrific circumstances, is really beyond reason, or of any form of basic decency. The third section was to be for interviews of the bereaved. The infamous questioning and interrogation, which focused on the amount of alcohol consumed, whether or not the loved one had a ticket, and the time that they had arrived in Sheffield. The coroner visited that area and was perfectly happy, content and completely satisfied with the way the operation had been carried out. Later on that Saturday evening, at around 9:30pm, the identification process could start.

Yet worse was to follow. A decision so unbelievable, so awful, so vile, it goes well beyond the realms of comprehension. The then coroner, Stefan Popper, in consultation with senior police officers, insisted on blood-alcohol tests on the dead being carried out to find the levels of alcohol on those that died. Why would such an ill-thought, wicked, unparalleled decision like this be taken? After all, it would not happen, has not happened at other major disasters. It was the mind-set of that time of football hooliganism, which was at it's peak, which in the eyes of Thatcher and her cronies, that excessive drinking went hand in hand with soccer violence. The self serving police, whose abuse of powers were well known and documented at that time were only too happy to go along with this idea and wholeheartedly adopted this policy. This was Thatcher's Police State. Yet, many people, up and down the country, at sporting events and other special occasions, quite readily consume alcohol. At international and domestic rugby matches, test cricket, The Open Golf Championship, Wimbledon, The Grand National and Royal Ascot, the Boat Race, Henley Regatta, in the theatre, opera, The Last Night of the Proms, the list is endless. Yet, if you are a football fan and you consume alcohol you are automatically labelled as a thug or a hooligan. A view that is stereotypical in the extreme, and a convenience in order to pass on the blame. At Hillsborough, this prejudiced view and convenient thought was all part of the cover-up, of fabrications and lies and of falsehood, just to shift the blame. Dr. Popper has a lot to answer for in his role during the aftermath of Hillsborough and beyond. It all comes to down to the connecting influences of Hillsborough, and who was to blame. Firstly, South Yorkshire Police and their poor mismanagement of the day, and a match commander with little or no experience of policing a major sporting event. A force that showed little in the way of care or control, and senior officers who froze. The decision of Duckenfield to open the gate, and then as Lord Justice Taylor put it 'a blunder of the first magnitude' when the entrance to the tunnel was not closed off and fans were not directed to the less full side pens. Secondly, Sheffield Wednesday Football Club. The Green Guide – Guide to Safety at Sports Grounds, revised and republished in 1986, gave detailed guidance on safety measures at football grounds. The Health & Safety Executive (HSE) in their findings into the disaster revealed that Sheffield Wednesday Football Club breached Green Guide recommendations. Furthermore, Lord Justice Taylor commented on Sheffield Wednesday's overall responsibility as 'occupiers' and 'inviters' and how they breached The Green Guide and contributed to congestion outside the stadium and the eventual disaster inside it. The Taylor Report confirmed that 'congestion at the turnstiles was foreseeable and that the club knew best what rate of admission the turnstile could manage, and they (Sheffield Wednesday) should have alerted South Yorkshire Police to the likely danger of crowd congestion.'

Thirdly, Sheffield City Council. The council were responsible in regard to issuing a new safety certificate for Hillsborough Stadium. The certificate should have been amended to take into account the changes to the ground. Lord Justice Taylor stated, 'the certificate did not take into account the alterations made to the ground in 1981 and 1985. A number of breaches to The Green Guide standards were permitted, and failure to revise the certificate allowed for such breaches, such as the spacing of crush barriers, the width of emergency exit gates and the gradient of the tunnel to persist.'

Fourthly, the Football Association. The FA selected Hillsborough as a 'suitable venue' for the semi-final not enquiring whether or not Sheffield Wednesday had the necessary safety certificate. The FA was roundly criticised by The Football Supporters Association, Liverpool FC and Lord Justice Taylor for the 'ill considered choice of venue.'

A lot of people, in a number of agencies had a lot to hide, and a great deal to lose regarding Hillsborough. The police, who lost the plot, knew that they were in deep trouble and that senior officers had cocked up, screwed up, f***** up, use whatever terminology you like. The initial, blatant lie by Duckenfield got them off the hook.

Sheffield Wednesday Football Club had breached a number of Green Guide recommendations. They should have also foreseen the congestion outside the stadium, and the danger that it caused. Yet, that lie by Duckenfield could get them off the hook.

The fact that Sheffield City Council had not revised the safety certificate for the stadium, despite changes being made to the ground on two separate occasions in 1981 and 1985, contributed to the disaster in relation to crush barriers, exit gates and the tunnel gradient. Again, the blatant lie could get them off the hook.

The Football Association, in a monumental error, did not enquire if Sheffield Wednesday had a valid safety certificate. This gross negligence contributed to the disaster. The blatant lie told to Graham Kelly by Duckenfield was convenient for the FA Chief Executive, and to believe it would get the FA off the hook.

All very convenient, and the basis for a cover up ensued. All parties were perfectly happy for Liverpool fans to take the rap. A central figure in all of this was Stefan Popper, the then Sheffield Coroner. A man who worked for Sheffield City Council, one of the agencies at fault in relation to the disaster. A man who met with senior police officers that April evening. I can safely say that you would not need to be a fly on the wall in that meeting to know what was discussed and what action would be taken. The blatant lie by Duckenfield had taken centre stage. A lie that would have such an effect on the future events that transpired and would force the bereaved families and survivors to defend the dead time and time again. To actually have to go through the trauma and grief of losing loved ones at a major disaster, followed by the insensitive way in which the identification process took place, and being told that 'the body belongs to the coroner not you,' is surely bad enough for anyone to take. But then to defend your own loved ones against all the wicked lies, fabrications and falsehood, over many years, from different people in many quarters – successive governments, police, the press, politicians, writers and ill-informed or prejudiced members of the public – the vast majority of whom were not even at Hillsborough that April afternoon, is something almost too much to bear. I, myself, have learned over the years to answer these accusations with a lot more maturity. I know the TRUE facts, after all I was there. How the bereaved families have coped with this, and have indeed kept their dignity, is beyond my thinking. I am a survivor, I did not lose anyone as regards a relation at Hillsborough. However, I did lose 96 friends, yes, fellow Reds, and I think about them, and pray for them each and every day. I cannot imagine what I would have done if I had lost a father, mother, brother, sister, wife, son or daughter that day. Those families are a group of the most wonderful, tolerant, patient, respectful, unwavering people that you could ever wish to meet. They are the best of human beings who will never WALK ALONE.

Chapter Five

Lies, Damned Lies

In the immediate aftermath of any disaster a process of the official line of what happened is released to the public and the press are always eager to get to the story and of the true facts. Sadly, there have been far too many disasters in this country in modern times that we know about all too well, whether it be Hillsborough, Piper Alpha, Lockerbie, the Bradford Fire, Marchioness, Herald of Free Enterprise, the Kings Cross Fire, the Clapham rail crash et al. This was known as the 'disaster era' when so many tragedies took place in a relatively short space of time, between 1985 – 1989. Then there are the recent tragic events such as the Cumbria Shootings. All terrible disasters, which brings about much pain to the bereaved relatives and indeed, to the survivors. The extensive media coverage can be very intrusive and difficult to take or handle.

The official line and what was actually the truth of what happened at Hillsborough is somewhat different. It was a ticking time-bomb ready to explode, a powder keg lit by Duckenfield's deliberate lie regarding the gate. The crass and vile decision of the coroner to order blood-alcohol tests on the dead, set minds alert to the fact that drink was involved. After all, this was a football match and it involved Liverpool fans, who, four years earlier, had played a major part in the Heysel tragedy, some said, quite wrongly, that it was all down to them. Yet, Heysel and Hillsborough were two totally different tragedies. The thought was put into peoples minds that this was drink related, that ticketless thugs had forced open the gate and killed their own fans. A lie of convenience. This was evident in the totally degrading and disgusting questioning of relatives who had come to identify their lost loved ones in the gymnasium at Hillsborough, which was used as a temporary mortuary. The questioning that went along the lines of 'how much did he/she have to drink?' or 'was he/she in the possession of a ticket for the match?' and 'what time did they arrive in Sheffield?' Can you imagine what state of mind you would be in if you were asked questions like that after your loved one had died in such horrific circumstances and you were there to identify the body? It is just unbearable. The fact that those relatives reacted with such dignity under those conditions of vile accusations at a time of deep grief is an amazing feat of total self control.

The fact that South Yorkshire Police set the tone and pointed the finger of blame squarely at Liverpool fans, many of whom they claimed were drunk and ticketless, meant that the media would report this version of events. Graham Kelly, the FA Chief Executive, was told by Duckenfield that fans had forced open the gate, so he naturally passed this message on to the waiting media, who were eager for a story. Furthermore, Graham Mackrell, Sheffield Wednesday Secretary, reiterated this point. Another report suggested that the gate had been broken down by a large number of ticketless fans. Yet where was all this evidence? As we all know, there was no such evidence.

It was plainly obvious that South Yorkshire Police were perfectly happy with their version of events. It would get them in the clear and they would be innocent of any wrong doing. All very cosy. The media were reporting all of this to the public at large, who in turn were quite happy to blame 'those Scousers' again.

In the press conference that took place that evening, the then Chief

Constable of South Yorkshire Police, the late Peter Wright, commented on 'four thousand Liverpool fans arriving five minutes before kick off. ' I know for a fact that the statement made by Peter Wright was a complete and utter lie. You could not get 4,000 fans down that narrow bottleneck of Leppings Lane at that time – 2:55pm. The whole area was already jam packed well before that time. I also mentioned the absolute FACT that a senior officer asked for the turnstile gate to be opened to relieve the pressure. As we know, this has been proven time and again.

The media frenzy intensified in the next hours and days. A city in mourning, families in mourning, survivors in mourning. Yet, the blame on Liverpool continued, unabated. A disaster within a disaster. It was not just the media, however. A number of local MP's and members of the government launched disgraceful and scathing attacks on Liverpool fans, as did the then President of UEFA, Jacques Georges. He stated that Liverpool fans were like 'beasts charging into the arena.' He later had to retract his diabolical statement. One of the worst verbal assaults, however, was reserved for the then Press Secretary to the Prime Minister, Bernard Ingham. A true rabid, right-wing Thatcherite, he voiced that Liverpool fans were 'a tanked up mob.' How did he know? How did any of them know? After all, they were not there. Nor did they witness the full horrors in front of them, or had to try to fight for their lives to get out of the hell hole that was the killing fields of Leppings Lane.

The press and the media in general were very eager to report the so-called 'facts' to the British public. So what were those facts? The fact that Duckenfield lied. The fact that many fans tried to heroically save lives and used their own initiative in relation to pulling down advertising hoardings and using them as makeshift stretchers. The fact that these fans tried to give the kiss of life, and offered support to the injured, and those traumatised like myself. In truth, fact never came into it, but falsehood did. The falsehood of drunk and abusive fans, of ticketless thugs trying to force their way in no matter what, of Liverpool fans killing their own. This falsehood dominated the media coverage from Sunday morning onwards. Even The Sunday Mirror, which has often supported our cause for JUSTICE stated that 'several thousand Liverpool fans were seemingly uncontrolled.' Even TV news coverage, by both the BBC and ITN, criticised Liverpool fans for 'impatience' in getting to the match. Unsurprisingly, local press coverage rounded on Liverpool supporters. The Sheffield Star was roundly critical. It's front page headline talked of 'a race to the stadium.' It said of 'up to 40 people died in the tunnel.' How did they know this? The fact was that the vast majority actually died in pens 3 and 4. The Manchester Evening News, always happy and willing to have a go and slag off Scousers reported that 'many fans charged the terrace without tickets.'

The Police Federation, naturally, had to stick the boot in too. Their spokesman at the time, a person by the name of Paul Middup, reiterated Bernard Ingham's false claim of a 'mob tanked up on drink.' He went on to say that 'officers were put in a frightening situation.' I would like to ask Mr. Middup what sort of situation the Liverpool fans, the survivors, and especially the 96 that lost their lives that day, were placed in? How frightening was it for them?

Yet all of these lies were to take a more unpalatable, nasty turn as the days went on. The Sheffield Star went at it without remorse once more, in defending their police force and roundly blaming Liverpool supporters, without any basis of evidence. They stated that the police had allegations that Liverpool fans had committed deplorable actions on the 15th of April. A story that these fans had attacked rescue workers and had stolen from the dead. If this had been the case how come they were not arrested? A further revelation of falsehood centred on 'drunken fans attacking police.' Again, why were they not arrested? It went further, when the paper stated that 'ticketless thugs had staged the crush at the turnstiles to gain entry to the ground, but these yobs had attacked ambulancemen, firemen, and punched and urinated on policemen as they gave the kiss of life.' All absolute lies and falsehood. A local newspaper trying to protect it's own and has never even had the courage or the bottle to apologise.

Of course we all know that things were to get even worse, even more disgusting and disgracefully vile with the press and media coverage. Most notably, of course, with The S*n and it's sickening headline 'THE TRUTH.' The Truth? That gutter rag wouldn't know the truth if it smacked them square on the jaw. Of course, the man who thought up this headline of lies, Kelvin MacKenzie, is hated and despised on Merseyside and by all Liverpool supporters, and is it little wonder? The former editor of THAT newspaper actually wanted to use an even more inflammatory headline, 'YOU SCUM.' He changed his mind. Yet, the deliberate lies and fabrications featured in The Sheffield Star the previous night, hit the national press the next morning, most starkly of course, in The S*n. The disgracefully wicked 'THE TRUTH' headline was followed by 'fans picked pockets of the dead,' and 'fans urinated on brave cops,' and 'fans beat up PC giving kiss of life.' Again, I will reiterate, where is all the evidence? Why were these 'fans' not arrested? Other newspapers followed suit, but it was The S*n and Kelvin MacKenzie who received all the anger from Merseyside. To this day, that newspaper sells hardly any copies in Liverpool and Merseyside in general such was the anger felt. A footnote to all of this, and a very unsurprising one at that, is the fact that a lot of the quotes in the press coverage actually came from sources within The Police Federation. Another instance of cover up, lies and falsehood. Not only had 96 men, women and children lost their lives, and hundreds of fans been injured, with thousands traumatised, now the grief stricken, bereaved families had to defend the dead against false allegations and absolute lies. The public perception being that Liverpool fans were to blame, through drunkenness and ticketless yobs charging the gate.

The people of Liverpool, and of Merseyside, are an amazing people. They are very resolute, resourceful, loyal, generous, clever and of course, funny. When the tide is against them, and the back is against the wall, they fight their corner, they show that Churchillian Dunkirk spirit. They will not be bowed, nor defeated. This can be said about what happened after Hillsborough. The national tide was somewhat against them. The whole era of the 1980's and Thatcher's Britain was not a good time, especially on Merseyside. A virtual police state, a laissez-faire ideology. A concept of 'greed is good,' the right to strike virtually taken away. The rich got richer, the poor got poorer. On Merseyside, thousands lost their jobs and were thrown on the scrapheap. It was obvious that Thatcher hated Merseyside and wanted to destroy it. But this great city would not be destroyed. Neither would it let the lies and the fabrications and the cover ups surrounding Hillsborough go unpunished. The REAL TRUTH would come out. The search for JUSTICE started that fateful sunny April afternoon. There have been many setbacks along the way, as well as some victories. Yet, still we fight to put an end to these falsehoods, these fabrications, these injusticies, and these LIES, DAMNED LIES.

Chapter Six

Miscarriages of Justice

It is often said regarding the judicial system in this country that everyone 'has their day in court.' That the law is there to protect the innocent, and to prosecute the guilty. Regrettably, that does not always happen. There has been, over the years, a list of miscarriages of justice that have been shocking to the extreme. The Birmingham Six and the Guildford Four immediately spring to mind. Yet, those involved were convicted of something that they did not do, and were later acquitted and pardoned. As regards Hillsborough, those responsible were never convicted in a court of law for something which many held them accountable, and the fact that there is hard evidence to convict them. All in all, Hillsborough is quite simply the biggest miscarriage of justice in the history of the British legal system. Furthermore, 23 years on, the families of the 96, and the survivors, are still fighting for justice.

The tone was set that fateful Saturday afternoon the 15th of April 1989. Again, we return to the initial lie by Duckenfield. It set the wheels in motion, the wheels that drove the term 'miscarriage of justice' to a sickening new depth. The law, the British judicial system, has badly let down the victims families and the survivors time and time again, and at every turn. If that is not a gross miscarriage of justice then I surely do not know what is.

The following day, Sunday the 16th of April, the British people woke up to the terrible and heartbreaking realisation that one of the worst disasters ever to hit this country had happened the day previously. It was also Britain's worst ever sporting disaster, and over 90 people lay dead, that figure would rise to 95 in the coming hours and days (the 96th victim, Tony Bland remained in a PVS – Persistent Vegetative State – for a number of years). This was a time of deep grief, especially on Merseyside, yet it seemed that most of the country was in mourning, unable to take in what had happened. At times of national tragedy, a lot of prominent V.I.P's visit those affected, whether they be politicians, royalty, or in the case of Hillsborough, footballers. The Prime Minister often takes the lead in such matters and visits the injured survivors in hospital and tours the area where the tragic events took place. Often an entourage accompanies the Prime Minister. This happened following Hillsborough. It was decided that Margaret Thatcher would visit the injured at Sheffield's two main hospitals – The Royal Hallamshire and Sheffield Northern General. This is the same Prime Minister who despised Liverpool and it's people. The same Prime Minister who brought a city to it's knees and created an underclass. The same Prime Minister who brought much misery and poverty to a once proud industrial area and threw thousands upon thousands onto the scrapheap. Hardly the most ideal person you would want to see by your hospital bedside after suffering terrible injuries in a horrific disaster. There was this notion that here stood a caring, sympathetic Margaret Thatcher visiting the injured, offering support. Yet, almost in the same breath, she was with her entourage, including Bernard Ingham, who stated that 'a tanked up mob caused the disaster,' and her Home Secretary, Douglas Hurd. They visited the stadium that same day, stood by the buckled safety barriers, visited the tunnel, viewed the ripped down fencing and surveyed the killing fields of Hillsborough. Also there that afternoon was the then Chief Constable of South Yorkshire Police, Peter Wright, who had rounded upon Liverpool fans during a press conference the previous night. It would not take much guessing what would have been said in private. There you had a Prime Minister who hated football, despised the city of Liverpool, a Press Secretary who blamed the disaster on Liverpool supporters, and a Chief Constable who pointed the finger of blame squarely at the fans. I am also sure that Douglas Hurd would be compelled to tow the party line.

There were fans in those hospitals who, when knowing of Margaret Thatcher's impending visit, decided to sign themselves out of the hospital, despite being injured. They did not want to be a part of the farce of Thatcher's staged visit. Obviously traumatised, these fans did not want to be anywhere near a Prime Minister who, in truth, would not normally give those people the time of day. Furthermore, anti-Thatcher feeling amongst Liverpool fans was extremely rife at that time, for very good reason. There was mass unemployment, abject poverty and deprivation, and football fans were treated abysmally.

There were other visitors that day, most notably HRH The Prince of Wales. I am not what you would call a devout royalist, and I see some members of the extended royal family as leeches sucking on the gravy train, to get as much as they can without giving anything back. However, would it really be any better under a republic? After all, we would have to serve a president and his entourage. A different kind of gravy train. All things being equal, Prince Charles is a decent bloke. He works tirelessly and is always there it seems during a crisis or a disaster. He offers support and is sympathetic, understanding, caring and compassionate. If I had been in one of those hospital beds that day, I would certainly rather have Prince Charles visit me than Margaret Thatcher.

The Liverpool players also came to see the injured too, on the Monday. I know that meant a lot to those who were hurting so much, both physically and psychologically. The players themselves were traumatised and grief-stricken, but they did an amazing thing that day and many other days, they offered support to injured survivors and to the victims families. We all know how magnificent Kenny Dalglish was after Hillsborough. He was already a legend before it, our greatest ever player and successful manager. But after Hillsborough he was just top class and beyond compare. In fact they all were. A number of the players made tape recordings for fans, who were in comas. I do not think any of that support will ever be forgotten.

The following day, after Margaret Thatcher had made her publicised and staged visit to Hillsborough, Douglas Hurd, the Home Secretary, ordered a full inquiry. It was to be led by Lord Justice Taylor. He seemed to be the right man for the job, having a keen interest in football. His brief was plain and without fuss – to look into the events of Hillsborough on the 15th of April 1989, and to recommend the needs of safety and crowd control at sporting venues. Everyone eagerly awaited the findings of The Taylor Report, from the bereaved families and survivors, to South Yorkshire Police, the coroner, the Football Association, Sheffield City Council and Sheffield Wednesday Football Club. A lot of very interested parties. What Lord Justice Taylor had to say would surely impact on future court proceedings and in the inquests of those that died at Hillsborough. It was expected that the truth about the disaster would come out and South Yorkshire Police were confident that the enquiry would show them in a good light, that they would be vindicated and what they said about crowd misbehaviour, drunkenness, and ticketless thugs who would stop at nothing to gain entry, would be the absolute true fact.

On the 28th of April 1989, less than two weeks after the disaster, Lord Justice Taylor held a preliminary hearing to set a date for oral evidence to be heard involving those interested parties. These interested parties were:

1. The bereaved and injured from the disaster
2. South Yorkshire Police
3. The Football Association
4. The Football Supporters Association

5. Sheffield Wednesday Football Club
6. Sheffield City Council
7. South Yorkshire Fire & Civil Defence Authority

Lord Justice Taylor's Interim Report makes interesting reading, which was dated the 1st of August 1989. The report talked of 'some fans drinking but not excessively, but a lot of public houses were closed to football supporters.' Any off licences in the area reported 'not to be overly busy with fans.' A special train carrying some 300 Liverpool supporters arrived at Wadsley Bridge station at about 2pm. They were escorted by police to the ground. The behaviour was 'good natured.'

As time went on, the build up in Leppings Lane became more intense, there was 'frustration and some anger,' and a beer can was thrown at a mounted police officer. Hardly major drunkenness. There was a 'major problem developing regarding crowd build up. ' Many fans complained to police officers about the seriousness of the situation. Superintendent Marshall realised' that 'the crowd had become unmanageable.' He requested that Gate C be opened.' Duckenfield was considering the request. In truth he was dithering and 'he (Duckenfield) froze.' The match commander was not in control of the situation when he needed to be. Eventually, Duckenfield gave the order to open the gate at 2:52pm. Around 2,000 fans entered, the vast majority with tickets for the terraces, some had tickets for the stand. 'A large proportion of fans headed straight for the tunnel in front of them,' the report stated. It talked about the steep 1 in 6 gradient, and also insisted that the tunnel should have been closed off, like it had been the previous year. The conclusions that were drawn up in The Taylor Report clearly laid the blame at the hands of the police, specifically with senior officers.

In the section 'BRIEF SUMMARY OF CAUSES' the report states that 'the immediate cause was gross overcrowding' and that 'the disaster was a failure to close off access to the central pens which were already overfull once Gate C had been opened.' Furthermore, the report stated, that 'the Operational Order and police tactics on the day failed to provide for controlling a concentrated number of large numbers.'

Lord Justice Taylor stated in his report that 'the main reason for the disaster was failure of police control.' He also commented on the oral evidence given by some 65 police officers. He stated that 'Sadly, for the most part, the quality of their evidence was in inverse proportion to their rank.' He went on. 'There were many young constables who were intelligent, open and alert. They inspired confidence and hope.' Yet, he was scathing of senior officers. 'The senior officers in command were defensive and evasive witnesses. Neither their handling of problems on the day nor their account of it in evidence showed their qualities of leadership expected with their rank.'

Lord Justice Taylor was damning in his criticism of the match commander, Chief Superintendent David Duckenfield. He stated 'Mr. Duckenfield lent heavily on Mr. Murray's experience. Between them they misjudged the build up of the turnstiles and did little about it until they received Mr. Marshall's request to open the gate.'

Furthermore, the report stated 'Mr. Duckenfield's capacity to make decisions and to give orders seemed to collapse.' Lord Justice Taylor was also scathing of Duckenfield's decision to pass the blame onto the fans. The report speaks of 'He gave Mr. Kelly and others to think that there had been an inrush due to Liverpool fans forcing open a gate. This was not only untruthful. It set off a widely reported allegation against the supporters that caused grave offence and distress.' In concluding, Lord Justice Taylor stated that 'He (Duckenfield) froze.' The report was particularly graphic in it's description of the dead. It shook me to the core when I first read it. It states that, 'what they found was a horrific scene of carnage. It was truly gruesome. The victims were blue, cyanotic, incontinent, their mouths open, vomiting, their eyes staring. The scene was emotive and chaotic as well as gruesome.' Truly awful. I witnessed this, so did many others. It is something which has haunted me for the past 23 years. It is certainly true that you learn to cope, almost accept it, but it tends to control your life, and you never actually get over it.

One crucial paragraph in the report centred on the conduct of the fans. The same fans that the police rounded upon and blamed for the disaster. The report said, 'Many fans also worked prodigiously in attempts to revive the dead and dying, in some cases their own relatives or friends.'

It went on to say, 'Then the fans improvised by tearing down the hoardings around the edge of the pitch and against the stands so that lengths of board could be used as stretchers. Improvising in this way, parties of fans and police repeatedly ran the length of the pitch bearing casualties to the north-east corner.'

Truly heroic. It could hardly be described as the work of a 'tanked up mob' could it? Yet, Duckenfield set it all in motion by stating that it was the fans who caused the disaster. The Taylor Report produced evidence that totally refutes that, and the finger of blame was laid squarely at Duckenfield and senior officers within South Yorkshire Police. The most scathing comment in the report was reserved for Duckenfield, after he had ordered to open Gate C and did not advise for the tunnel to be closed off to deny access to the central pens – Pens 3 & 4. Lord Justice Taylor stated, 'It was a blunder of the first magnitude.'

The report sent shockwaves through the entire country when it was first announced. The police, who thought they would be vindicated by blaming the fans, had a new problem. The Taylor Report had the view that the main cause of the disaster had been serious failures by senior officers of South Yorkshire Police, insisting that 'lack of care and control had been the root cause.' The fans were exonerated. In fact, they were praised for their general behaviour and for their heroic rescue attempts to save lives. The fact that drink and drunkenness was not a major issue, nor was the notion that ticketless fans had caused the disaster. In fact, ticketless fans at Hillsborough was not a major issue. The report gave substantial evidence to support this. A fair number of witnesses spoke of the fact that the side pens were sparsely populated, as was the North Stand, quite close to kick off. This pointed to the fact that quite a large number of ticket holders remained outside the ground, and they could account for the large build up outside. Furthermore, the club's own electronic monitoring system and analysis undertaken by HSE (the Health & Safety Executive) suggested that no great number of ticketless fans entered the stadium. Furthermore, the Health & Safety Executive, in it's own independent findings stated, 'the numbers of persons inside the Leppings Land end on the afternoon of Saturday the 15th of April 1989, did not exceed the numbers of tickets sold for that area on that day.' A victory for the bereaved families and for the survivors, albeit a hollow one.

Yet, The Taylor Report did not go as far reaching as the bereaved families and the survivors would have hoped. There were several fatal flaws to the report. This is a great pity, because in the referral about the causes of the disaster, and the gross mismanagement of South Yorkshire Police, it was spot on. Despite this, Lord Justice Taylor praised the force for their previous 'good works.' This included The Miners Strike of 1985. Hardly something to be congratulated about. There was much bloody violence inflicted during that time, much of it perpetrated by the police in an effort to make the striking miners submit. A virtual police state. This was Thatcher's Britain, and the abuse of power at it's very height. The fact that police officers were given huge overtime bonuses, and miners and their families were starving, having to survive on meagre strike pay and reliant on donations by members of the public is sickening to the extreme. Furthermore, the police had the authority to 'go in hard' and this they did, sometimes with great relish.

Furthermore, there was no mention of the horrific situation with the identification process. The vile questioning of bereaved relatives, the rushed identifications, being forcefully stopped from spending a little time with their loved ones – 'the body belongs to the coroner, not you.' The blood-alcohol tests were mentioned, but with no criticism of this denial of basic human rights. The report mentioned the levels and how many had been drinking. In truth, it was not that many, over half of those that died had not been drinking at all, and those that were, in most cases, the amount of alcohol consumed was 'negligible.' There was no criticism of SYMAS (South Yorkshire Metropolitan Ambulance Service) and the fact that a fleet of some 44 ambulances stood idle outside the stadium, as fans lay dying. There was no mention of this, and despite criticism from two doctors, one who went on national television, the emergency services, said Taylor, 'responded promptly when alerted.' In fact, Taylor criticised the doctor for going on national television, calling it 'irresponsible.' Why was nothing mentioned about the fleet of ambulances outside the stadium and that so few ambulances made it onto the pitch? That a police officer had told ambulance drivers that "You can't go on the pitch there is crowd trouble, they are fighting." The true facts were that of the 96 that died at Hillsborough only 14 made it to hospital. More could have been done to try at least save the dying fans. Yet, Taylor talked of 'little more could have been done for them.' A man with no medical background or experience came to this glaring and false conclusion, but on what basis?

Whatever the shortcomings of The Taylor Report, and there were many, what is indisputable is the fact that Lord Justice Taylor, a renowned High Court judge, pointed the finger at the police, specifically senior officers as regards the Hillsborough Disaster. Furthermore, drunkenness, ticketless fans, or hooliganism, played no part in the tragedy. The notion that they, the fans, had caused the disaster, started by Duckenfield's lie, had no basis in truth whatsoever. So where could the police go from here?

They had to, publicly at least, accept the findings of The Taylor Report. This did not, however, hide the fact that they were extremely unhappy about the ruling given. There was the offer of resignation by South Yorkshire's Chief Constable, Peter Wright, a man who had rounded on the fans previously. He did so again, stating that 'the inquests would give a different account of the disaster and reveal the true, full story of what happened. His officers would be cleared of any wrong doing. ' The basis was there for yet more lies, more fabrications, more cover ups. The inquests would be a sham. After all, Popper had a lot to lose, as did Wright, as did Duckenfield and Murray. It could hardly be expected that the inquests would be wholly impartial, as the coroner, Dr. Stefan Popper, who would lead the inquests, had ordered blood-alcohol tests on the dead. It smelt of bias and prejudice from day one. A Sheffield coroner, in a Sheffield court, who worked for Sheffield City Council, and a disaster that happened in Sheffield. A coroner who had ordered blood-alcohol tests on the dead, who had, in conjunction with senior police officers, insisted on the temporary mortuary at the gymnasium and the vile questioning of relatives, already distraught and grieving, which focused on the time of arrival as well as the amount of alcohol consumed, and whether or not they had a ticket. A rushed identification process where the relatives were told that 'the body belongs to the coroner, not you.' A lack of sympathy and understanding and a denial of basic human rights. Yet, Popper was 'perfectly happy' with this process.

It is usual for inquests to be opened and then adjourned. It is deemed as normal practice. This allows for bodies to be released for funerals. This was the case following the Hillsborough Disaster. Furthermore, coroner's courts only deal with death, whether it be accidental death, suicide or unlawful killing. It is also a place which brings much grief and trauma, and the re-opening of old wounds. Not a very pleasant experience. Another point worth noting is the fact that the coroner's court is often the last chance that bereaved families can get to find some kind of justice, or answers to fundamental questions, often if they feel badly let down by criminal cases or civil proceedings. It is imperative, therefore, that the coroner shows a certain willingness to offer empathy, understanding, sympathy and respect. This was sadly lacking at the Hillsborough Inquests.

There was also a further wait for the inquests to begin. The DPP (Director of Public Prosecutions) was still waiting for the final report from the West Midlands Police in their investigations into the Hillsborough Disaster and whether any criminal charges should be brought. Yet, Popper chose not to wait, and took the unprecedented decision to begin proceedings through mini-inquests for each of the deceased. They would then be adjourned in order to wait for the DPP's decision on prosecution. These individual mini-inquests would deal with the medical evidence for each of the deceased, the precise location before death, identification and, amazingly, and with sickening prejudice, the blood alcohol levels. What possible reason did the coroner have to bring up the issue of blood-alcohol tests, tests which he ordered, in conversations with South Yorkshire Police?

This is hardly impartial in relation to the inquests. Another dubious scenario also developed. On the 6th of March 1990, Popper held what was termed as a 'pre-inquest review meeting' with Mervyn Jones, the then Assistant Chief Constable of West Midlands Police. This was the man who was responsible for the coroner's investigation into the disaster. Also present were so-called 'other interested parties' represented by solicitors. A cover-up ensued. It was decided that no controversial issues would be addressed. Why? The bereaved died in controversial circumstances, so why should controversial questions not be asked. Another clear indication of a 'fit up.'

The inquest into the biggest sporting disaster in British history were about to take place. Yet, there would be no controversial questioning, it would be a strictly limited inquest. The emergency services would not be present – police, fire and ambulance services, as well as rescuers, doctors and nurses. All very comfortable and convenient. The fact that officers from West Midlands Police, a force deep in controversy and indeed infamous in certain quarters, would give oral evidence to the inquests, which was pre-selected, all sat very well with the coroner. The lack of impartiality was mind-blowing. Furthermore, there would be no opportunity for cross-examinations to take place, nor the chance to challenge anything as regards evidence. There was nothing for the bereaved families, or indeed, the jurors, to question. A total sham. A blatant cover up.

The coroner then wrote to the families in regard to a date being set for the mini-inquests to begin. In a stunning, yet awfully crass decision, the date set for commencement of proceedings was the 18th of April 1990, just three days after the first anniversary of the disaster. What a diabolical decision to make. The fact that the bereaved families would be in deep grief, virtually on the first anniversary of losing their loved ones in the most horrific of circumstances, did not seem to weigh on Popper's mind one iota. Maybe it did. Maybe it was a deliberate ploy, knowing full well that those families would be in no fit state emotionally to attend the mini inquests. A way to find a weakness, to kick them when they were down. It would not surprise me one little bit if that were the case. Yet, those families showed tremendous courage in the face of this awful adversity, and attended those mini-inquests.

As time got nearer for the mini inquests to begin, the families knew little or nothing of what to expect. It was natural to think that way. After all, inquests are such a terrible ordeal they are usually over with very quickly. Yet, they were nervous with what to expect, what would come out, what the police would have to say, who were none too happy regarding The Taylor Report, which firmly lay the blame for the disaster at their door.

So, the mini inquests began, with several selected witnesses called. A Dr. Forrest, who was a chemical pathologist, gave evidence regarding blood-alcohol levels. The obsession with the police, in conjunction with the coroner, and certain sections of the media, was of drunken behaviour being the direct cause to the disaster. Yet, this had been wholly disproven by The Taylor Report. Still, they hammered it home. In a totally despicable statement, one of the families own solicitors, a man by the name of Doug Fraser stated that, "About a sixth of those that died were too drunk to drive."

What a totally stupid, grossly moronic and insensitive thing to say. The families were now battling against members of their own legal team as well as South Yorkshire Police and the coroner. The media were only too happy to report this. Whilst some newspapers reported the days proceedings fairly and without bias or prejudice, it was left to The S*n to round upon Liverpool fans again, as they had done following the disaster. A crass headline that read, '15 Hillsborough Dead Too Drunk To Drive.' The article went on to comment that '51 of the dead had been drinking.' Yet, actually how much? If you look at the levels properly you will see in the main they were negligible, and in fact half of the dead had not touched a drop of alcohol at all. The notion that 15 were too drunk to drive could mean what? It would mean that they were over the legal limit to drive a vehicle, which could be anything from 1 – 3 pints of lager or beer, or 2 – 3 glasses of wine. Hardly overly excessive drinking. Instead of the policy of blood-alcohol levels being questioned and challenged, the mini inquests sought to justify this policy, which in truth, is both indefensible and lacks any sort of basic human rights. The bereaved families had to defend their lost loved ones yet again. The popular myth of drunken, ticketless thugs causing the disaster had reared it's ugly head once more. Of course, there was no opportunity to challenge evidence during the mini inquests. The evidence remained as it was presented and was uncontested. The bereaved relatives had some burning and crucial questions that needed addressing, but Popper would not allow it, there were a lot of interests to protect, and people with an awful lot to lose. Therefore, a gross miscarriage of justice took place during those mini inquests. But that was only the start of a judicial process that would let down the bereaved families, the survivors, and most importantly, the 96 who lost their lives at Hillsborough. A system that has protected the guilty, and those in authority, for over two decades.

A letter that was dated 30th August 1990, which was written by Mr. Cleugh, who was at that time Head of the Police Complaints Division, to the Chief Constable of South Yorkshire Police. It stated that after careful consideration of all the evidence and documentation, the Director of Public Prosecutions has decided that there is no evidence to justify criminal proceedings against South Yorkshire Police, Sheffield City Council, Sheffield Wednesday Football Club and the safety engineers. Furthermore, there is insufficient evidence to proceed against any officer within South Yorkshire Police. Another gross miscarriage of justice. The bereaved families now had only one avenue left open to them, that of the coroner, for them to have their unanswered questions addressed and to get to the bottom of the whole affair. Margaret Thatcher had got her way. After all, she had stated, following the disaster, 'I do not want any policeman prosecuted over Hillsborough.'

The full inquests were opened on 19th November 1990. The venue was Sheffield Town Hall, and they lasted for four months to 28th March 1991. There was evidence taken from 230 witnesses, and the inquests were the longest in British legal history. There was representation for several parties, twelve in all, and six senior police officers were also represented. There was no representation for survivors of the disaster, like myself. There was no legal aid afforded which I find to be totally disgusting. Another clear indication of the judicial system badly letting down Liverpool fans, survivors, the bereaved families, in regard to Hillsborough.

The way the inquests were run was another indisputable fact that they were not wholly impartial, or without bias and prejudice. In a decision that is beyond any realms of sensitive thought and regard for the bereaved and the survivors, the coroner insisted that no evidence would be given in regard to events after 3:15pm on the day of the disaster – in other words a self imposed '3:15pm cut off' policy was adopted by Popper. Why was this unbelievably awful decision reached? After all, there was no basis for this decision. There was no evidence to suggest that all the victims were brain dead or had no chance of life by 3:15pm. The basis that Popper used for this decision was that there were St. Johns Ambulance personnel on the pitch, and nothing more could be done for the victims. Yet, there is evidence to suggest that more could have been done, and fans could have been saved.

When I read Anne Williams' very moving and extremely touching book entitled **When you Walk Through the Storm** it truthfully brought me to tears. As a survivor of Hillsborough, I knew what happened there that day, after all I witnessed it. I was part of it. I saw bodies on the pitch and felt them beneath my feet. Yet, there was a lot I didn't know, such as what happened to Anne Williams' son, Kevin, who lost his life at Hillsborough. He was just 15 years of age. Yet, Kevin could have been saved, and there was evidence to prove it. There were also witnesses. The fact that Kevin was alive after 3:15pm and uttered the word 'Mum' before he died is indisputable evidence that the 3:15pm cut off insisted upon by Popper was wrong, proving the inquests were a farce, a sham, a cover up. These witnesses were never called to the inquests. It was all selective, all at Popper's discretion. It was fine to have paid off local residents and selected licensees, but to have a Special WPC who was with Kevin when he died, as well as another PC, an ambulance driver, and a CCTV technician, all of this concrete evidence was simply not on in Popper's eyes. There were a lot of interests to protect. There were also people with a lot to lose, such as police officers and their more than generous pensions.

Debra Martin was recruited as a Special WPC in 1987. The role of a 'Special' is somewhat different to that of a regular police officer. Their work is more voluntary, and they are employed in other jobs. In Debra Martin's case, she worked as a dental nurse so she had some medical background and experience. She also had experience of policing matches at Hillsborough, and was present at the semi-final the previous year.

As the horrors unfolded that sunny April afternoon, Debra Martin was completely unaware of what was to confront her. She spoke of an ambulance trying to gain access to the pitch, of police officers stood there doing nothing, bewildered and in total shock, of the dead being grey in colour. She offered help by taking the injured to the gymnasium, Debra talked of fans vomiting, of broken ribs and of death. There were some who had blood in their mouths, and nothing could be done for them. As Debra worked tirelessly to try to save fans, her medical background proving invaluable, she was asked to try and help Kevin Williams. Debra stated that Kevin started to look grey but there was some colour present. She stayed with Kevin and continued to work on him, trying to find a pulse at the back of his neck. Eventually, Debra found what she describes as a 'slight blip.' She continued to try to save Kevin through heart massage and mouth to mouth resuscitation or 'the kiss of life.' She stated that his chest expanded a number of times. Debra held him in her arms and Kevin opened his eyes before uttering the word 'Mum.' He died at 4pm.

After Kevin had died, Debra Martin was ordered to stay with him. She was told that 'nobody else could touch the body.' As it turned out, not even bereaved relatives. An absolutely sickening procedure. Eventually, Debra went to the new Medico-Legal centre in Sheffield, where she had to give details about the body. There was a lot of paperwork to get on with. Inside that Medico-Legal centre, Debra described a scene where bodies were being stripped and clothes piled up in a corner, in which she said it was 'like something from Auschwitz.' For a police officer to describe a scene like that, is undeniable proof of the callous way in which the dead, the bereaved and the survivors were treated. There was absolutely no dignity for the dead. No basic respect for the body.

Around three weeks later, Debra Martin made her first written statement. It was pretty much what she had written in her pocket book. Later on, she was visited by two officers from West Midlands CID, who wanted to make sure that Debra got 'the evidence right.' She was pressured by one officer, a WDC Julie Appleton, who claimed that 'another off duty officer had found Kevin.' A week later WDC Appleton came to see Debra again. At the end of the interview she was coerced and bullied into signing a new statement. This was a common procedure in police statements given following Hillsborough. Many were changed and altered, words omitted and sentences changed. A pre-meditated plan to get senior police officers off the hook and to blame the fans for the disaster. As it turned out, Debra Martin was not called to give evidence at the inquests. This seems, on the face of it, to be rather strange that a police officer, who was with one of the victims, who comforted him and tried to aid him, who had medical experience, who heard Kevin utter the word 'Mum' at nearly 4pm, was not called to give evidence. The evidence being that Kevin was alive up to 4pm, that he was not brain dead at the 3:15pm cut off point, that he spoke before he died. Yet, it was a deliberate ploy of the part of the coroner who played an active role in this whitewash. He was still alive up to 4pm, and was able to speak before he died, uttering the word 'Mum' before he passed away.

There were other witnesses who were not called to the inquests. They had crucial evidence to give in relation to the cut off point and the rescue policy of the emergency services. There were also pathologists who contradicting the evidence given by Dr. Slater, a Rotherham pathologist, who stated that Kevin had the worst injuries of any that died at Hillsborough. The injuries were so severe, he would not be able to speak. It was claimed by Slater that Kevin had a number of fractures to his voice box, thus not allowing him to talk. He added that Kevin looked blue in colour, yet when Mrs. Williams viewed her son he did not appear that way.

In her search for the truth surrounding Kevin's death, Anne Williams sought the advice of an eminent forensic pathologist by the name of Dr. Ian West. He was based at the world renowned Guy's Hospital, London.

He had undertaken autopsies on a number of controversial deaths, and was a leading light in his specialist field. He would be what can be termed as an 'expert witness.' He disagreed with Slater's findings. The neck injuries could not be described as 'fatal.' Furthermore, Dr. West came to the conclusion that Kevin Williams could have survived well beyond 3:15pm. He also stated, which totally contradicted Slater's assertion, that a dead body never twitches, convulses or moves in any way. If that were the case it was more likely to be a body that was still alive and not one that was dead. A stunning piece of evidence. Another expert, Dr. James Burns, from The Royal Liverpool Hospital, reaffirmed Dr. Ian West's testimony and explained the specifics behind Kevin's injuries. He also went on to say that if a simple tracheotomy had been performed it could have saved his life. Yet, it was like a lot of victims at Hillsborough, little was done for them when much more could have been done. If more had been done, and if the emergency services had done their jobs properly, many lives could have been saved.

PC Derek Bruder was an off duty Liverpool policeman who was at Hillsborough on the 15th of April 1989. He was sat in the North Stand. He saw all the horrific events unfold before his very eyes. He also tended to Kevin Williams on the pitch. He noticed a lot of policemen stood there doing nothing to help the injured and dying, though he stated that some officers did an awful lot to help. That is not in dispute. It also emerged that PC Bruder wrote a statement regarding what he had witnessed at Hillsborough. He was contacted by officers from West Midlands Police and pressurised into altering that statement. The altered statement was the one read out at the inquests.

Tony Edwards was the only ambulanceman to get onto the pitch at Hillsborough that fateful April afternoon. Whilst there were some 44 ambulances waiting outside, Tony Edwards' ambulance was the only one to get onto the pitch, breaking through the police cordon. It was denied by South Yorkshire Police that any ambulance made it onto the turf, but CCTV proved otherwise. Another blatant LIE by the police. Tony Edwards said of what happened, "A policeman stopped us and told us that we couldn't go on because fans were fighting."

ANOTHER LIE.

Once he eventually got onto the pitch, what Tony witnessed changed his life forever. He stated, "The first thing we saw was Liverpool fans running towards us carrying an advertising hoarding, the type you see round the edge of the stadium, but they were using it like a stretcher."

In the end, the ambulance was full of as many bodies it could take, so Tony decided to pull out. No other ambulances replaced his. Tony was told by his bosses that he was 'too emotionally involved because he was from Liverpool.' It was their part in the mass cover up that followed Hillsborough. Eventually, Tony Edwards left the ambulance service through Post Traumatic Stress Disorder. The questions have been with him for over 20 years, and it still gets to him today. Tony is still angry that senior police officers covered up their mistakes with blatant lie after lie. He said, "Why were there 44 ambulances not allowed on the pitch? Why was there only one ambulanceman on that pitch? I don't believe that those questions have been answered properly, even after 20 years. There are people who have been dishonest."

Roger Houldsworth was the video/CCTV technician at Hillsborough. He maintained the equipment in the police control room at the stadium. At the inquests, Mr. Houldsworth, predictably, was not called to give evidence. Yet, the police claimed that the equipment was faulty and that senior officers, including Duckenfield and Murray, could not get a clear picture of the crowd build up in the central pens – Pen 3 & Pen 4. Mr. Houldsworth has always disputed this. He stated, "Firstly, there was the camera that wasn't working. I proved it was working. Then there was the interference from the Outside Broadcast unit. But if that had occurred it wouldn't have affected just one camera, but all five. All their excuses were inaccurate to say the least."

Mysteriously, if that is the right word, on the night of the 15th of April 1989, two video tapes, which filmed the horrific events unfold, went missing from the police control room at Hillsborough during a 'break in.' Nothing else was taken. It does not take a genius to work out what transpired. Someone in the know, in authority, knew that the evidence on those tapes was incriminating. Those tapes had to be got rid of.

Despite all the evidence of Special WPC Debra Martin, PC Derek Bruder, Tony Edwards and Roger Houldsworth, they were not called to give evidence. The two changed statements of the police officers involved were offered at the inquests. Yet more damning proof of the cover up between South Yorkshire Police and Popper. Furthermore, the role of West Midlands Police in all of this cannot be underestimated. A police force surrounded with controversy, shrouded in corruption and thought of with deep mistrust. Their role in the conviction of The Birmingham Six is well known. Yet, those men were found innocent and had their convictions quashed. But that is only the start. There is a catalogue of abuses of power perpetrated by officers from West Midlands Police, most notably The Serious Crime Squad. One such case was that of Keith Twitchell, who served 12 years for robbery and manslaughter. He eventually had his conviction overturned by the Court of Appeal. Mr. Twitchell remembers to this day the details of what happened to him. He stated, "They put a bag over my head and it was clamped tight around my eyes and mouth. I remember struggling and heaving but I must have gone unconscious." Keith Twitchell later signed a confession. The methods were described to the Court of Appeal as 'a scenario of torture that beggars belief.' A forced confession that led a man to serve 12 years in jail for something he did not do. Keith Twitchell's account is just one in a long list of wrongful convictions that have come to light involving West Midlands Police. So far 30 convictions have been quashed by the Court of Appeal because of evidence that the squad fabricated, such evidence as that of tortured individuals and forced signed confessions. On the

14th of August 1989 (four months after Hillsborough) the Serious Crime Squad was disbanded by Geoffrey Dear, the then Chief Constable of West Midlands Police. An investigation was set up by the 'independent' PCA – Police Complaints Authority – and was conducted by West Yorkshire Police. The PCA investigation looked at 97 complaints against The West Midlands Serious Crime Squad, made between January 1986 and August 1989. Between March 1990 and October 1991 the inquiry passed a succession of files to the CPS – Crown Prosecution Service – to 'consider' criminal charges against some of the officers concerned. By this time, the Birmingham Six, who had been convicted of the IRA pub bombings in 1974, had been freed by the Court of Appeal in which officers from the squad had played a significant part. Their actions had been shown to be 'flawed.'

In May 1992, the then DPP – Director of Public Prosecutions – Dame Barbara Mills, decided that there was 'insufficient evidence' to prosecute any single officer. The PCA, in it's final report, published in January 1993, stated that officers within The West Midlands Serious Crime Squad were 'working unrealistic hours.' Officers were 'abusing the overtime system,' with some working 100 hours overtime every month, mostly for visits to licensed premises to 'meet contacts.' The official report made no mention of the 'plastic bagging' and other torture techniques referred to by the many victims whose convictions have now been quashed by the Court of Appeal. Another instance of a gross miscarriage of justice. A police force, then, that would be hardly fit to offer a fair and balanced report into the Hillsborough Disaster, and to submit evidence for the inquests that should be totally and wholly impartial and without prejudice or bias. As we know today, this was not to be the case. The inquests were not impartial, nor were they fair, or without any prejudice or bias. They were, without question, a deliberate and well-planned stitch up.

Furthermore, and appalling in the extreme, part of the investigating team into Hillsborough, was none other than Detective Superintendent Stanley Beechey, the head of the now disbanded West Midlands Police Serious Crime Squad. Here was a man who was under investigation, yet he was part of the investigating team, and was often at the side of the coroner, Dr. Stefan Popper. His role was a very significant one. The fact that this man was even still in the police force, let alone be part of the team that was investigating Hillsborough and the process of gathering evidence, is truly beyond belief. A police unit that had been disbanded, a police unit deep in controversy and corruption, a police unit that had fabricated evidence, tortured victims to sign statements and had planted forensic evidence. Yet, the head of that unit was now part of the investigating team. The tone was set.

The West Midlands Police team which investigated Hillsborough, had been given a brief to 'restore confidence in the police.' Yet, not many people had confidence in The West Midlands force. The team's investigations centred on South Yorkshire Police and their role in the Hillsborough Disaster. They also provided evidence that went to the DPP – Director of Public Prosecutions – who decided that there was 'insufficient evidence' to bring about a prosecution. Furthermore, the investigating team provided and 'selected' evidence that went to the Coroners Court. They also acted as Officers to the Coroner during the inquests. People were then visited and re-visited in order to get a 'clearer picture' of the events. Survivors were severely pressured and bullied, so much so some even doubting their own experiences of Hillsborough. This same tactic was used on police officers like Special WPC Debra Martin and PC Derek Bruder, forcing them to alter their original statements. A familiar tactic used by The Serious Crime Squad of the West Midlands Police, though, admittedly, in a more severe way. Yet, it was quite clearly a tactic of intimidation, bullying and coercion. There was a hidden agenda in place, in order to 're-write Hillsborough' for the purposes of the inquests. It was, without question, all part of the cover up regarding

Hillsborough. Everything was now set in place for the most controversial inquests in British legal history.

From the outset, the focus of the inquests centred on drinking, drunkenness and ticketless fans. It was as if those that died at Hillsborough, their bereaved families and the survivors, were on trial. It was supposed to be an inquest in relation to how those that lost their lives actually died, the cause of death, where they died and at what time they died. The inquests were supposed to give the jury a balanced and fair account of what happened that day so that they could come to a decision in their deliberations and give a verdict, whether it be unlawful killing or accidental death. Those inquests were neither balanced nor fair. The selective witnesses, such as hand picked local residents and publicans, whose evidence was flimsy to say the least, if not wholly untrue and full of discrepencies. The unbelievable decision by Popper and the '3:15pm cut off point' for evidence. The role of West Midlands Police in the investigation and the leaning on of witnesses to change statements. The blood-alcohol tests on the dead read out with 'fifteen being too drunk to drive.' What about all of those that had not been drinking? What about those that had negligible amounts of alcohol in their bloodstream? What does 'being too drunk to drive' actually mean? In plain, commonsense, it tells me that those would be over the legal limit to drive as I have mentioned previously. This could mean that they had consumed between 1 – 3 pints of beer or 2 – 3 glasses of wine. Hardly what you would describe as a huge amount of alcohol.

The inquest verdicts when they came were of no surprise to many. The fact that Popper, in his summing up of deliberations and directions, made it quite clear that in the letter of the law that a conviction of unlawful killing in a criminal context can be described as involuntary manslaughter. He used the word recklessness as a basis, which had to be proven beyond all reasonable doubt. As regards a verdict of accidental death, the coroner instructed members of the jury that the word accident involves completely all the events that unfolded and that something that nobody had control over and therefore nobody could be blamed. The jurors were told that if they were satisfied that there was carelessness or negligence then someone would have to make payments of compensation in civil litigation. He went on further, talking of this verdict not absolving all parties from blame. Yet, Popper continued to reaffirm the crucial words 'negligence and recklessness.' He was trying to make the dubious point that recklessness and negligence were not compatible, that they were not the same, that they were totally different. Furthermore, Popper kept forcing home the point that the jury had to be sure beyond all reasonable doubt for an unlawful killing verdict. The fact that Popper was instructing the jury in this way, and that if there was any doubt at all in their minds, telling them that the only possible verdict that they could come to was accidental death, really spoke of those two crucial words which I have used before 'bias' and 'prejudice.' The fact that the coroner instructed the jury to reach a verdict of accidental death proves what a cover up and a total sham those inquests were. And so, on the 28th of March 1991, almost two years since the disaster, the jury returned a verdict of ACCIDENTAL DEATH with an 11 to 2 majority verdict. Naturally, the bereaved families and survivors were left devastated. They had been let down by the British judicial system and by the coroner's court. A coroner who was all part of this elaborate whitewash, who made crass decisions regarding the inquests, who knew full well of the consequences if a verdict of UNLAWFUL KILLING had been returned, had got what he and South Yorkshire Police had wanted, and yet had been part of a gross miscarriage of justice. And with no prosecutions being granted by the DPP due to 'insufficient evidence,' the bereaved families not only felt betrayed and let down, they were now also at their lowest ebb.

As it has been said many times, the bereaved families, the survivors, have never given up in this seemingly endless fight for justice. Without doubt, that takes an immense amount of courage, patience and great resolve. Some two years after the inquest 'verdicts' were announced, six of the bereaved families sought a judicial review of those inquest verdicts. In seeking a judicial review, those families did so under Section 13 of the 1988 Coroner's Act. There were to be test cases for those that died. The families gained a significant victory in winning leave to challenge those verdicts of accidental death. The consent for a judicial review was given by Mr. Justice MacPherson who stated that 'the case had a sensible basis for argument.'

The judicial review opened a year and a half later in the Divisional Court. There would be two judges present to hear the case, Lord Justice McCowan and Mr. Justice Turner. The barrister representing the families, Alun Jones QC argued strongly that there had been bias in the original inquests and that evidence had been withheld or suppressed. Naturally, those representing the coroner dismissed such claims. The judges ruled in favour of the coroner. A case of 'looking after their own.' They even went as far as to say that the inquests had been run in a correct manner and that there was no suppression of evidence, and, amazingly praised Popper. Even more controversial in the judges decision was after hearing strong medical opinions from two eminent pathologists, who contradicted Dr. Slater's testimony at the inquests, their 'version' was dismissed. We are talking about two leading lights in their field, Dr. Ian West and Dr. James Burns. Yet, their conclusions counted for nothing. Such as victims could well have survived well after 3:15pm, which was offered by Dr. West. Furthermore, Dr. Burns gave his opinion that even in severe cases of traumatic asphyxia, death does not necessarily occur in three of four minutes, the victim could survive for a considerable period of time. It, was therefore, not certain that all those that died did so within three or four minutes. Yet, what these two eminent medical experts had to say was totally dismissed. Another miscarriage of justice.

The families and the survivors would have to wait another four years for any hope of getting some kind of justice. In 1997, a new government was elected. A new government, with fresh ideas, and the same deep-rooted cover ups and miscarriages of justice. Yet, there was some renewed hope when Tony Blair's New Labour came to power. Perhaps things will be different, thought many, as regards Hillsborough. Maybe, just maybe, someone was listening. I, myself, as a survivor, and a lifelong Labour supporter, had some new optimism despite all the previous setbacks. I was of the firm opinion that previously it had been the despised and hated Tories who had helped to cover everything up and under Labour things would be refreshingly different. Was I really that naïve?

However, optimism was high when Jack Straw announced that there was to be a judicial review or scrutiny that would be wholly 'independent.' What those in authority call 'independent' and what I would term in the same language would be somewhat different I suspect. Yet, leave had been granted by the Home Secretary that gave everyone some renewed hope, even if there was some scepticism. The man appointed to lead the independent judicial scrutiny was an Appeal Court judge by the name of Lord Justice Stuart-Smith. His remit was to scrutinise and consider any new evidence that may have come to light. Yet, there were severe limitations and boundaries to the scrutiny. It was only to look at new evidence, and evidence not given before the Taylor Inquiry, to the DPP, the Attorney General and South Yorkshire Police and it's Chief Constable. Early optimism gave way to serious concerns, and doubts were cast to what the scrutiny could actually achieve. The fact that such limitations were put in place paints a picture of things being swept under the carpet yet again. Surely, the bereaved families deserved a scrutiny that set no limitations, that did not adopt boundaries. The fact that the inquests were a sham, that witnesses were not called, that statements were changed through bullying, intimidation and coercion, speaks volumes.

The scrutiny did have one positive for the bereaved families. The realisation that files on the deceased which had been held at South

Yorkshire Police headquarters under lock and key, were now available for them to look at. The indisputable fact that it had taken eight years for this to happen, however, is yet another example of the massive cover up of Hillsborough. Those families should have been able to view those files from the outset, not wait nearly a decade. When those files did come into their domain, they proved what the families suspected – the statements within those files had been tampered with and altered.

When Lord Justice Stuart-Smith met with some of the bereaved families on the 6th of October 1997, outside the Maritime Museum in the regenerated docklands area of Liverpool, he made a statement that was beyond comprehension, and reason. A statement so insulting, disrespectful and vile, it sent shockwaves through those present. He stated, "Have you got a few of your people, or are they like Liverpool fans, always arriving late?" Yet again, the tone was set. He had it fixed in his mind that Liverpool fans arrived late at big matches, no doubt thinking that they were worse for drink, or did not possess a ticket. This was the man who the families had placed trust with in order to get some kind of justice. Naturally, the families were totally shocked and outraged by such remarks, yet they still kept their dignity. An apology was demanded and given, with Stuart-Smith 'regretting the remarks' and stating that he 'did not mean to offend.' But the damage had been done.

On that first day of proceedings in Liverpool, Stuart-Smith made it clear what he would consider as 'new evidence.' In his terms, new or fresh evidence would be 'evidence that was not available nor presented to previous inquiries, courts or authorities.' In his opening statement, Stuart-Smith was saying that the Taylor Report had been thorough and extensive, damages had been paid out by South Yorkshire Police, and the inquests had been described as 'exemplary' by the Court of Appeal. He was agreeing with everything that had gone before. Yet, this argument was fatally flawed as the families now had access to the statements for the very first time, which clearly showed that previous investigations were suspect, with statements altered and changed. Stuart-Smith dismissed this new evidence as inadmissible according to his 'terms of reference' and he constituted it as not being 'new evidence.' Yet another stitch up. He stayed in Liverpool for three days, taking evidence individually from sixteen families. The meetings were very formal and in some cases quite hostile. You would have thought with what those families had been through for the last eight years there would be some kind of understanding, sympathy and respect. It certainly was the case that Stuart-Smith was far from objective and fair in his approach. He considered these files as not 'new evidence' as they had been before other investigations. Yet, the families had not seen these files before and so it was new evidence to them. Without doubt, Stuart-Smith had a huge brush in which he swept everything under the carpet. A familiar story.

On the 18th of February 1998, the families travelled to London to meet Jack Straw, the then Home Secretary. He was to tell them the outcome of the scrutiny. Amazingly, he described Stuart-Smith's scrutiny as 'impartial and 'thorough.' Furthermore, he stated, 'nothing of any significance had emerged to warrant a new inquiry.' He totally accepted Stuart-Smith's findings calling them 'objective.' Another miscarriage of justice. Yet, the evidence was there, written in black and white. The evidence of statements altered and changed, the authorities could not deny that, but they could deny the families justice. It was a case of having too many interests to protect so let's cover it all up yet again. New Labour were just like the Old Tories. The promises made in opposition came to absolutely nothing. The promises of justice failed to materialise. The Stuart-Smith Scrutiny only served to highlight that the bereaved families and the survivors have not received any kind of justice following Hillsborough. It was a case of protecting those at fault, those who should have answered for their part in the deaths of 96 innocent men, women and children. The following is a statement from the summary of the scrutiny which is now a public document and can be viewed as such.

'I have come to the clear conclusion that there is no basis upon which there should be a further Judicial Inquiry..........

There is no basis for a renewed application to the Divisional Court or to the Attorney General to exercise his powers under the Coroners Act 1988. I do not consider that there is any material which should be put before the Director of Public Prosecutions or the Police Complaints Authority which might cause them to reconsider the decisions they have already taken........

I have considered the circumstances in which alterations were made to some of the self-written statements of South Yorkshire Police officers, but I do not consider that there is any occasion for further investigation.....'

Absolutely diabolical. The evidence was there in black and white, namely the changed statements. The fact that Stuart-Smith submitted boundaries and limitations in relation to evidence, is, if you pardon the pun, not playing on a level playing field. It certainly does not appear to be fair or balanced. The fact is, the families have not been given a fair or balanced basis for argument ever since the disaster happened. Another miscarriage of justice.

More than two years would pass before the bereaved families were to get another 'day in court' in pursuit of justice. The HFSG (Hillsborough Family Support Group) raised funds through a concert at Anfield, featuring The Manic Street Preachers and other acts. The money raised was to fund a court case – a private prosecution against Chief Superintendent David Duckenfield and Superintendent Bernard Murray, the two most senior officers on duty at Hillsborough on the day of the disaster. The Manic Street Preachers even wrote a song called 'South Yorkshire Mass Murderers.' The support for justice remained strong amongst the majority of the public, which was helped in no small part by Jimmy McGovern's excellent drama-documentary 'Hillsborough.' A number of television documentaries, most notably 'The Cook Report' had shed new light on the disaster. These programmes had high ratings and would stick in the public's imagination and psyche. So, in June and July of 2000, a trial was held at Leeds Crown Court. Finally, Duckenfield and Murray were in the dock, more than 11 years since the disaster. The judge for the trial was to be Mr. Justice Hooper. The two defendants, Chief Superintendent David Duckenfield and Superintendent Bernard Murray were each charged with two counts of Manslaughter, in that they both failed to prevent the crush after the gates were finally opened, and by failing to prevent access to the tunnel and failing to divert fans from the tunnel which led to the already full pens 3 and 4. A further charge of Misconduct in Public Office was also recorded against both defendants. Further charges were made against Duckenfield, a charge of Perverting the Course of Justice. However, this charge was dropped after the Attorney General intervened. The final charge recorded against Duckenfield was that of Misconduct. This came from the fact that he lied, claiming that Liverpool fans had forced open the gate when it was himself who had ordered the gate to be opened. During the trial, the charges were reduced to just one count of manslaughter. Yet again, those at fault were getting away with it and the families and survivors were being cheated out of justice.

During the pre-trial rulings, Lord Justice Hooper was asked to halt the trial by the defence barristers representing Duckenfield and Murray. How sickening and disgraceful a plan of action. The claim being that they (Duckenfield and Murray) would not receive a fair trial. What about the families? They never received fair inquests, nor was the judicial scrutiny a fair and balanced one. After much deliberation, Hooper decided that the trial would indeed go ahead, but under certain 'conditions.' The defence barristers were right about one thing – the trial was not fair. Not fair for the families or the survivors. He would not allow the infamous S*n article printed a few short days after the disaster, to be used by the prosecution during the trial. This ruling by Hooper allowed him to put a ban on any 'unwelcome' publicity, which might prejudice the trial.

He was helping out the defendants. He helped them out even more. Inexplicibly, Hooper decided that if convicted, Duckenfield and Murray should not go to prison. An unbelievable instruction. He argued that they would be 'at risk from serious injury or death' if indeed they were sent to jail. One law for one, another law for someone else. We were at risk from injury or death on the 15ᵗʰ of April 1989 when we went to a football match, and 96 of our brothers and sisters never returned home. I will refer to that much used term yet again – the tone was set.

The trial itself had several fatal flaws in how it was run. The HJC (Hillsborough Justice Campaign) has always maintained that it was, as they describe it a 'show trial.' I do have some sympathy with that notion. The fact that evidence heard would only be up to the time of 3:06pm – the time that the referee, Mr. Lewis stopped the match – is even more restrictive and obstructive than the coroner's 3:15pm 'cut-off point.' Why did the prosecution not challenge this? The fact is that evidence should have been heard up to 4:00pm. After all, there were fans still alive up to this point.

The first day of the trial sparked controversy and undeniable evidence that the families were being victimised and treated as criminals yet again. In a totally unbelievable piece of court 'theatre' and of insensitivity beyond belief, or of any degree of reasoning, Lord Justice Hooper called into court the police officer responsible for policing arrangements outside the court. Hooper stated, "We are all concerned about any protests or demonstrations which could affect the fairness of the trial." The policeman in charge went on to say, in a court of law, "There has been an issue today with a protest group and the police have been called." Where was this evidence of a protest group? The policeman certainly could not produce any. There was talk of leaflets and posters being handed out, yet none was forthcoming. The bereaved families were there at a trial where in the dock was Chief Superintendent David Duckenfield, the man held most responsible for what happened at Hillsborough. Those families were seeking justice, something that had not been afforded to them for the past 11 years. The last thing on their minds would be to hold a protest and hand out leaflets or posters. The finger was being pointed at distraught bereaved families and survivors, just as it had been at the fans at Hillsborough. The blame game. They were blamed for being 'demonstrators' or 'protesters.' Hooper even went on record to state, "You could be charged with breach of the peace or perverting the course of justice.' In his mind, these brave families, survivors, were seen as 'troublemakers' when all they wanted was some kind of justice. Towards the end of the trial, there really was a protest campaign, with leaflets being handed out. Those leaflets were read out in court, and were in fact a plea to halt the trial and stop the two defendants from being harassed. The leaflets came from the church next door to the court, yet the vicar denied any involvement when called. Amazingly, Hooper took no further action. There were no threats of court orders and the like, no mention of 'breach of the peace' or 'perverting the course of justice.' A sickening proof of the double standards and deep hypocrisy that was on show. It emerged that later on, leaflet after leaflet were left lying around inside that church. A vicar, a so-called Christian, lying in a court of law. As a Christian myself I am deeply appalled and ashamed. His Christian duty should have been to try and offer support and reassurance to those bereaved families and survivors, instead of instigating a vicious campaign of prejudice.

During the trial, the defence barristers, predictably, peddled their sick lies, the disgraceful myths, the diabolical fabrications, that the disaster was down to ticketless, drunken, violent thugs. Despite The Taylor Report and it's findings, despite the lack of evidence, despite the lie of Duckenfield, they still used that as a basis for the defence of Duckenfield and Murray. The witnesses for the defence were a few selected local residents and senior police officers. When does a youth urinating in a garden constitute several thousand drunken, ticketless thugs? The argument was flimsy to say the least.

On the other hand, the prosecution witnesses appeared to be much stronger. There was a survivor who told of his ordeal, a judge, Sir Maurice Kay, who was also a survivor of the disaster, and several good testimonies from police officers. A vital witness for the prosecution was Roger Houldsworth the CCTV/Video technician. He told of hearing a message on the police radio that stated that if a gate was not opened outside the stadium then people would be killed. He said he heard a reply 'open the gate.'

Further to the defence submissions, Duckenfield chose not to give evidence. If I were innocent, I would jump at the chance to defend myself in a court of law. As we all know, however, he was not innocent. So much was his guilt, Duckenfield could not take to the stand. Yet, he didn't have the slightest amount of bottle or courage, much like at Hillsborough, to even say sorry, or to admit his guilt. However, the defence carried on with this theory of drunkenness, of ticketless thugs intent to get into the stadium any way possible. If anything, the fans were pretty restrained amongst all the chaos and lack of organisation that was on show that day. Yes, there were some angry fans, and who could blame them. It was a struggle in that bottleneck and people were distressed, people were getting hurt, people were crying their eyes out. Many feared for their safety. The lack of a genuine police presence was the primary reason for such chaos and therefore, poor organisation and direction of fans. To blame the fans was wholly untruthful and false. The defence, and in particular, Mr. Clegg, who represented Duckenfield, came in for some scathing criticism from the prosecution. The fact that he called in some local residents to give evidence, which was distorted, untruthful and at times mythical, much of it having nothing to do with the disaster at all, was not painting the true picture. There was also severe criticism of the evidence offered by senior police officers, particularly by Mr. Mole, whose comments were described as 'disgraceful.' He spouted the familiar South Yorkshire Police line of 'drunken, ticketless thugs.'

Mr. Justice Hooper's role in all of this cannot be underestimated. Here was a man who acted as an advisor to the Crown Prosecution Service in relation to Hillsborough. The same Crown Prosecution Service who stated there was 'insufficient evidence' to proceed with any prosecutions. Although he offered to step down as the trial judge, this offer was rejected by the prosecuting counsel. A strange decision to say the least. As we have seen, regarding the trial, Hooper's 'performance' as the trial judge was somewhat suspect and certainly not wholly fair or without prejudice. We have more evidence of this during his instructions towards the jury. He had certain questions for the jury to consider before they could come to a verdict. These were:

* 'Are you sure that it was foreseeable by a 'reasonable' match commander that by letting people in through the gates that there would be deaths in pens 3 & 4?'

If the answer to this question was 'yes' then they had to proceed to and consider question two, which was put as follows:

* 'Are you sure that effective steps could have been taken to close off the tunnel? Yes?'

* 'Failure to take such steps was negligent as a 'reasonable' match commander would have done so. Yes?'

* 'With regard to the risk involved, the failure to take such steps led to the serious criminal offence of manslaughter.'

Hooper made the point that if the answer was 'no' to question one, then a not guilty verdict must be returned. Furthermore, Hooper stated to the jury regarding a guilty verdict and that of a criminal conviction, if it might send out a wrong kind of message to others in emergency situations. Hooper was more or less warning the jury that if they gave a guilty verdict it could have serious implications in a court of law as regards emergencies, and the reaction of the emergency services in future emergency situations. He was trying to get Duckenfield off the hook. He made it perfectly clear that Duckenfield would not face a re-trial as it would be 'oppressive' and a further trial would not be seen as being 'fair.' The words oppression and fairness smack of hypocrisy. The bereaved families and survivors have been oppressed and have not received any fairness for over 20 years. By this point of course, Murray had been cleared. Yet, the jury could not agree on a verdict for Duckenfield, despite the stitch up and the bias of Hooper. Whilst some may argue that he was not found guilty, it can also be argued that he was not found innocent either. At least some of the jurors had the decency and commonsense not to let him off the hook completely.

As bereaved families and survivors left court for the final time, inexplicably, and beyond any kind of reason or justification, West Yorkshire Police filmed them leaving court. Why? What was the purpose? The police claimed that a threat had been made against Duckenfield or that there could be some disorder. The blame game again. I think that I can safely say that Duckenfield is a very lucky man to have remained physically unscathed. As a survivor of the disaster, I can honestly say that I have felt like over the past 23 years of taking a gun to his head. I am sure many others have too. Yet such is the extreme dignity of the bereaved families, of the survivors, that this has never happened. The biggest miscarriage of justice in the history of the British legal system and the guilty continue to walk free. The families and survivors have never given up this fight for justice, showing great courage and determination against the odds, Against all the criticism, all the lies, all the fabrications, the taunts, the myths, the intimidation, and not least the massive cover ups.

Chapter Seven

Renewed Hope or Hidden Truths?

On the 20th anniversary of the Hillsborough Disaster, suddenly everything surrounding the tragedy became headline news. There was no doubt that the 20th anniversary was a significant one, and media coverage was intense. The memorial service on the 15th of April was broadcast live by several channels and the attendance figure of well over 30,000 was much larger than in previous years. To many, the 20th anniversary seemed 'special.' Yet, to the bereaved families and survivors, every anniversary is special. The media coverage was welcome because it meant that even after 20 years of injustice, the search for justice could be highlighted and that people in government could be reminded of what still was required, namely JUSTICE FOR THE 96. Whether anything would be done about it was a different matter.

On a personal level, I watched the memorial service on TV. I still could not face going, or openly talk about the 'H' word as I referred to Hillsborough. It was a fact that PTSD still controlled me somewhat. The bottling up process had lasted for 20 years, as had my attempts to push it all away, as though Hillsborough and my experiences of it had never happened. Yet, there was a sea change happening. After all, I was watching the memorial service on TV, so that was progress in itself. As

I watched the service my stomach churned, spinning round intensely like a washing machine. The butterflies floated around in the pit of my stomach. It was pretty hard to watch. It was emotional, it was moving, it was upsetting. Yet, at the same time it was uplifting and I felt a deep pride, tinged with sorrow. I told myself that I had to return to Anfield, my 'home' for so many years. I had pushed it away, rejected it for far too long. A week or so later, I went to Anfield to lay some flowers by the memorial. My wife, Deborah, accompanied me and we spent the day in Liverpool.

What raw emotion I felt watching the memorial service was most prominent when 'JUSTICE FOR THE 96' rang out from more than 30,000 voices as they drowned out the then Culture Secretary Andy Burnham. He had come to the service as a government minister, and he had something to say. A government minister had actually bothered to be there with the fans. Of course there would be deep scepticism. After all, successive governments, whether Labour or Conservative, had badly let down the bereaved families and survivors over Hillsborough. They were all part of the cover up. The fact was that Labour, whilst in opposition, voiced concerns over Hillsborough and were determined to 'right the wrongs,' and when elected they were going to do something about it. When new governments get elected suddenly things change. This happened in 1997 when New Labour was swept to power in a landslide victory. The new Home Secretary was Jack Straw. He promised us the judicial scrutiny. Which, in the end, was another whitewash, another cover up. Jack, the Man of Straw, actually did nothing for the bereaved families and the survivors over Hillsborough. He later became Justice Minister, or should that be INJUSTICE? In that role he ignored all the evidence regarding the Michael Shields case, an innocent man jailed in Bulgaria for an attack on a barman following Liverpool's 5th European Cup triumph in 2005.

There was criticism, not surprisingly, of Liverpool fans when they roundly booed Andy Burnham and drowned him out with cries of 'JUSTICE FOR THE 96' at the 20th anniversary memorial service. It was deemed as not being respectful in some quarters. It was needed at the time and it was in honour of the 96 that lost their lives at Hillsborough. The quest for justice had gone on, with various setbacks, for 20 years. It was not being disrespectful, it was telling the world that 'we will not go away until we get JUSTICE.' It might be true that Andy Burnham looked decidedly uncomfortable that afternoon. I make no apology for what my fellow Liverpool fans did. However, I must give the former Culture Secretary some credit. He stood there and took it, at least there was one politician who had the courage to go to the memorial service and stand there in front of more than 30,000 people and face their wrath. I salute Andy Burnham for that.

It was a few short weeks later, when Andy Burnham kept his word and that something needed to be done as regards Hillsborough. He was to set up an independent panel and all documents relating to the disaster would be released 10 years early – or 20 years too late – for the panel to scrutinise. It was a positive move, and it seemed like a politician was finally listening. Yet, unsurprisingly, there was deep scepticism. After all, there had been many false dawns before. The panel would be chaired by the Anglican Bishop of Liverpool, the Right Reverend James Jones. Another positive move? I'm not so sure. It was expected that the work of the independent panel would take up to two years to complete, so nothing was going to happen overnight. There was a warning too. This was not a call for a new enquiry merely a scrutiny of all the documents relating to the disaster. Not a very helpful statement. However, it was some kind of progress. The bereaved families, the survivors, even the general public would learn more about what happened following Hillsborough. Finally, if everything was released as it should be, ordered by the government, then this massive cover up would be unearthed. It gave for much renewed hope and optimism.

All of us with any connection to the Hillsborough Disaster, those that fight for justice, have been let down many times before. When the General Election was announced early on in 2010, there was a stark realisation that the Tories could get in again. The hated Tories. The government that was in power in 1989, who started this massive cover up, whose abuse of power was never more prominent. There was that genuine fear and real concern that 'things could change' as regards the independent panel. A new government was indeed elected. Yet, it was a Conservative-Liberal Democrat coalition that took power. The 'ConDems.' I waited with baited breath to see what would happen.

I was looking forward to watching the World Cup in South Africa. My appetite for football had returned. I had attended the 21st anniversary of the Hillsborough Disaster and even went to a couple of games towards the end of the season. I had a feeling that I was finally coming to terms with PTSD. So I watched the World Cup unfold with much relish. When England got knocked out, not surprisingly, and I heard that there had been not one arrest, it made me think of all the times, over the years, that the racist thugs who followed England, what shame and disgrace they brought upon the country. This made a pleasant change. Finally, it would seem, that hooliganism, the so-called 'English Disease' had been eradicated. What was not so pleasant was what I heard next. The new Culture Secretary, Jeremy Hunt, gave an interview on Sky News where he was proud of the fact that not one English fan was arrested. He spoke of 'the past being behind us, and the problems of Heysel and Hillsborough in the 1980's.' He was linking Hillsborough with hooliganism. That same old discredited myth that Liverpool fans caused the disaster, which has been proven, time and again, as ABSOLUTE LIES. This public school educated Tory from Surrey has no clue about Hillsborough. If he did, or if he had done some research, he would not have made such an idiotic comment. Naturally, he had to apologise for those remarks. Yet, that was not the end of the matter. A week or so later, according to reports in The Daily Mirror, the Department of Culture, Media & Sport commented that 'documents relating to the Hillsborough Disaster may be withheld,' and that Mr. Hunt was 'taking a fresh look at the issue.' There was a source from within that department who claimed that 'things are not so simple anymore.' This brought shock and outrage. I personally wrote to Mr. Hunt, as did many others, including Anne Williams (the mother of Kevin Williams who lost his life at Hillsborough). In a reply I received from the department, the response said, 'Mr. Hunt has already apologised for the remarks which were a mistake. He does not blame Liverpool fans for the Hillsborough Disaster.' There was no mention of the change of policy. I sent another response to his department regarding the change of policy. I never received a reply. No surprise there then. The cover up over Hillsborough goes on. Furthermore, Andy Burnham challenged the Speaker in the House of Commons regarding this issue saying that, "The people of Liverpool deserve the full truth of what really happened at Hillsborough and the courtesy of a minister of the crown to tell them what they are up to."

The Speaker agreed that if a 'change of policy' has been adopted on this issue then the minister concerned should make a statement before the House. None was forthcoming in this regard. However, there is more on Jeremy Hunt later on. More sweeping of things under the carpet, things that could be uncomfortable for those in power and in authority. The same old story as regards Hillsborough – the absolute and deliberate denial of justice to the bereaved families and the survivors. The sickening process of 'HIDDEN TRUTHS.'

Chapter Eight

When You Walk Through A Storm

This has probably been the hardest part of this account that I have had to write, even more so than the chapter on the day of the Hillsborough Disaster itself and my own personal experiences of that tragic day. This is all about the 23 years of hell that I have had to live through with PTSD (Post Traumatic Stress Disorder) and how it has controlled my life. Yet, somehow, I survived.

When you witness death at first hand, when you are close to bodies that have fallen, of people trying to fight for their own lives just like yourself, a deep sense of guilt envelops you and gets hold of you. Why them and not me? Why didn't I do something? Why did I not help them? Those questions I have put to myself many times over the years when I have relived the torture of Hillsborough. If only I had done certain things differently, if only I had reacted in a different way. A lot of 'if only's,' a lot of regrets. This hidden guilt has affected a lot of survivors from Hillsborough. I know, because I have talked to several about this, and it has affected me. I admire greatly those that day who acted as brave rescuers, who tried to save the dying and aided the injured, who ripped down advertising hoardings and used them as makeshift stretchers, who were heroes to a great many people. How they did all of that after what they had witnessed is beyond comprehension. I guess some people are made differently, and some have a deep resolve, an inner strength, some are weaker, more emotional, you might say. When these same fans are accused of being drunken, ticketless thugs, then that just brings your whole world crashing down. How dare they say those things? How can they make up those lies? How would any decent human being cling to that myth? But to say those things makes them not to be 'decent human beings.' There were an awful lot of emotional scars left behind after Hillsborough.

After I had got out of that horrific carnage of pen 4, and I wandered like a mindless zombie aimlessly on almost every blade of grass of that pitch, I felt so damned helpless. Why did I shake so much? Why did my legs feel like jelly? Why did my knees feel as though there were about to buckle and give way? I couldn't answer those questions back then. I can now. I was in deep shock and extreme trauma, the onset of PTSD. I had entered a different world. A darkness that would control my life and where there would be no sign of this morbid blackness ending.

That very first night really was the worst night that I have ever had to face. I touched upon it briefly in the chapter entitled *'The Hillsborough Disaster – Saturday the 15th of April 1989.'* As I previously mentioned, it was the worst day followed by the worst night. I dared not fall asleep during the brief moments that I felt I was going to fall asleep. I had a deep fear of impending death. I had witnessed so much death that day, my mind told me I was about to die myself. I had vivid images in my head of what I had experienced that day, the first of countless flashbacks. There was much crying, and the intense pain of my bruised chest, stomach and back, and hurt ribs, meant the intense physical pain kept me from sleeping anyway. It was just the longest night in my entire life, as I lay there in that bed going over everything time after time.

The next morning there was just an eerie silence. It was the 16th of April 1989, the morning after the Hillsborough Disaster. In many ways it was the start of the grieving process, a time to mourn. As if you had lost a member of your close family in tragic circumstances, but almost one hundred times over. A truly awful, mind numbing experience. There was still a deep, intense rawness of emotion inside of me, quite naturally. After all, I had been part of the worst sporting disaster in British history. I ached all over as I painfully climbed out of bed and got dressed. I could not get the previous day's events out of my mind. Other people rang me to see how I was but I just didn't want to talk. As soon as you switched on the television or tuned into the radio everything was about Hillsborough. It seemed as if normal programming had been cancelled, but you would expect that under the circumstances. A major tragedy had rocked the nation and there had been many deaths, almost one hundred. Naturally, there was a deep state of shock and it appeared that the nation 'mourned.'

I watched the TV coverage intently, almost to obsession. It was getting a firm hold of me. It kept showing footage of the ground at Hillsborough, of the buckled barrier in pen 3, of the ripped down fencing and of V.I.P's arriving in the city, most notably Prince Charles, as well as the Prime Minister, Margaret Thatcher and her entourage. I could stomach just about anything, but not that woman and her false sympathy. The hated Thatcher, the destroyer of the fabric of society, the war with the Miners, her hatred of the unions and socialism, her laissez faire ideology. No thanks.

As the days slowly passed by, I just could not get my head round what happened at Hillsborough. I had handed in a sick note at work and so the days were long and restless. I was in this awful encased shell of withdrawal. Then, when I heard on the TV news about THAT headline in The S*n 'THE TRUTH' I just completely flipped. This was on the Wednesday. My body still ached to a mind blowing intensity, and now the finger of blame was to point to us. The focus, instead of being one of support, understanding, respect, was now one of 'killing their own,' 'robbing the dead,' 'urinating on corpses,' 'beating up cops.' I was totally inconsolable. The previous night, or it might have been on the Monday, I arranged with my friends that we should go to Anfield and lay some flowers and scarves and pay our respects. It is something that had to be done, but it was something that I was so frightened of doing as I did not have the stomach for anything connected with football. The 15th of April 1989 and Hillsborough had shattered me completely. It had ripped me apart beyond all recognition. Yet, it had to be done. I just had to be in Liverpool, I had to be at Anfield with fellow survivors, and people who understood our grief, what we had been through. As we walked around Anfield, I sensed how busy it was. There were an awful lot of people paying their respects, just as there had been the few days previously, since the Sunday. The queues stretched all the way from the Shankly Gates through the car park and right on to Walton Breck Road. We had to wait what seemed like a lifetime.

Gradually, the queue lessened as we got nearer the Shankly Gates. Eventually, we arrived by the big gate, which led into the Anfield Road End only to be told that nobody else would be let in. I was so emotional at this point. In a stupidly crass and insensitive comment, Edward, who was one of the friends I was with at Hillsborough, stated, "We have been here long enough, let's go," or words to that effect. I don't know how I managed to stop myself from smacking the life out of him, but somehow I did. Sharon, another of my friends who was there on the Saturday, was having none of this. She went up the steward on the gate and explained that I had been injured at Hillsborough and had been in the central pens and that I needed to go inside the ground. The steward relented and let us in. We were amazed by what we saw. A carpet of flowers, scarves, football shirts, hats and caps. The pitch was virtually covered. I had wanted to lay my flowers and a scarf on The Kop, at the bit of terracing where I stood each and every home match, but I couldn't such was the volume of tributes. I laid my tribute on the pitch, as did the others. I believe, thinking back, that Edward waited outside. Maybe he couldn't take it. Maybe he was in his own kind of grief and bewilderment. Who knows? I just thought he was an uncaring, callous soul. There is nothing that could have kept me from that pitch that night, and laying down my tribute. Absolutely nothing.

I was born a Roman Catholic. I was baptised, received first Holy Communion and was confirmed in the church. Yet, like many before me and since, I drifted away from church life, even from faith itself. This happened when I was 16. It seemed all so irrelevant back then. Some may see it as mere coincidence, but during my time away from God, from Our Lord Jesus Christ, from the Holy Spirit, awful things happened in my life. Yet, I never stopped believing. Maybe that is why my faith was renewed many years later. Following Hillsborough, I somehow needed some kind of interaction with the church, even though I had drifted away. I contacted my local priest, Father Patrick Keane, at Saint John the Baptist Roman Catholic Church, in Burnley. I told him about what had happened to me at Hillsborough. He was very compassionate and understanding, a truly wonderful parish priest. Father Keane offered to say a Mass of Remembrance on the following Saturday. It was a wonderful gesture and the church was full that day. I can certainly say that it helped me, initially, through that very difficult time. Sadly, Father Patrick Keane passed away early in 2010 in his native Ireland, after a long battle with cancer.

There came a time post Hillsborough when there had to be a return to some degree of normality. That included a return to playing football for the Liverpool team, even though it seemed so insignificant after what had happened on the 15th of April. The indisputable fact is that those players went through an awful lot as well speaks volumes. They were there that fateful day, they comforted the bereaved, they visited the injured and dying, they attended funerals and then they were expected to play football again. They were true heroes. I doubt whether I could have played football after what those guys went through, and I doubt whether many others could have too. The first game they played was a friendly match at Parkhead against Celtic, which was to raise funds for the Hillsborough Disaster Appeal. This was the first time that the team had played a game of football since Hillsborough. The game was won by Liverpool 4 – 1 in front of more than 60,000 fans, with goals from Kenny Dalglish, John Aldridge (2) and Ian Rush. The friendship, love and respect shown by Celtic fans that day will never, ever be forgotten. I didn't go to that game, nor the first two competitive games that followed – the 0 – 0 draw with Everton at Goodison Park on the 3rd of May, nor the 'replayed' FA Cup Semi Final with Nottingham Forest at Old Trafford several days later on the 7th of May, which Liverpool won 3 -1. After that, the feeling being I was ready to go back to watch football again, I didn't miss any more matches up to the end of the season. The emotional FA Cup Final, fittingly, against Everton, at Wembley hit me hard, but so did the joy, tinged with deep sadness, of winning that trophy for all those that lost their lives at Hillsborough. Of course, the final league game of the season six days later on a dramatic Friday night at Anfield, will go down in history as footballing folklore. Only seconds from a second league and cup double in three years, snatched away from us. I cannot blame the players, however. They gave their all over those last few weeks of the season with a fixture backlog and the emotions of Hillsborough still raw in the memory. They could have done no more.

The following season, I was back at Anfield, renewing my season ticket and went to all the home games, and a few away, though not as many as I had done in years previously. After Hillsborough, travelling to away matches didn't seem right somehow. It appeared as if I was recovering well, certainly on the surface, but deep down I wasn't. I was not facing my demons it must be said. I used drink to put things to the back of my mind – drink and anger. A very potent cocktail. The PTSD was really beginning to kick in and take a firm hold of me. Those that tell you that alcohol helps you forget about problems in your life are totally wrong.

It does not. In fact, it makes things worse. A whole lot worse. At that point in my life, however, I thought that booze did help me to cope with PTSD.

RETURN TO HELL

One away game that I did go to was when I went back to Hillsborough for the league game against Sheffield Wednesday in the November. A return to hell. A return to Leppings Lane. Those pens and that terrace had been closed off. The fences permanently ripped down after The Taylor Report recommendations. I had to sit in the West Stand above. It was a truly awful experience, but was something that had to be done. I went with the others – Sharon, Lynn and Edward. I could not help but look down into that unused terrace, that several months earlier had almost taken my life. It was not like attending any other football match I had ever been to before. It wasn't really a football match it was more of a tribute to those that lost their lives.

We travelled by car to Sheffield, arriving early. We had arranged to meet the wonderful couple, who took us into their home and offered us much needed support that April afternoon. We arrived about lunchtime and headed straight for their home, which was located on a council estate near Wadsley Bridge, just up the road from Hillsborough. After greeting them with flowers we all went to a nearby pub for a spot of lunch and a few bevies. I was trying to block everything out of my mind – the 15th of April, the dark tunnel, pens 3 & 4, all the death I witnessed, wandering around the pitch, and my total fear of returning to Leppings Lane for the match that coming evening.

As evening approached there was a growing feeling within myself of deep trepidation. A real fear surrounded and enveloped me. I had to revisit that ground where previously I had seen much death, much carnage, much horror. I had to walk down Leppings Lane again and I thought, oh God no, I don't think I can do it. I was shaking violently from the inside and my stomach churned. I felt physically sick. But I couldn't let them down, the brave souls who died that day. No way. I had to be strong. I had to go to that game. The walk to the ground was a horrible one. The nearer we got, the worse I felt. I resolutely held onto the hand of Sharon and Lynn. They had some good points about them, of that there is no doubt, especially that night. I had a bunch of flowers with me, which I wanted to lay on that empty terrace. As we turned into Leppings Lane, a deep blackness, a mind numbing grief came over me. I was back in that bottleneck which ultimately led to the deaths of 96 people. The girls held my hands tighter, realising how upset I was. We approached the entrance, which thankfully was further up that street and away from Gate C. I really did not want to go through that gate again. I would not have to go through that tunnel either, which was a blessing. As I recall, it was a November night but it was not that cold. Yet, there was a freezing shiver about my body. The next few moments, I nearly lost it completely. The police patrolled the entrance to the turnstiles. These same policemen were probably on 'duty' if you can call it that, on the 15th of April, a few short months beforehand. As I tried to enter the turnstiles, I was stopped by an officer. "You cannot take anything inside." His tone was unforgiving. I tried to explain to him that it was a bunch of flowers and the significance of it all. But he should have known that. The crass, unfeeling insensitivity was beyond understanding and reason. He still would not let me in with those flowers. I completely lost all reasoning and told him that I was going in with those flowers whether he liked it or not. It was just a bunch of flowers that I wanted to lay as a tribute. He could arrest me if he wanted, but there was no way that I was going to let this odious, uncaring little shit of a South Yorkshire police officer stop me from paying my own personal tribute. I rammed it home that his 'lot' had caused enough damage and enough heartache and had killed nearly 100 innocent people. By this time, several people had gathered, as had another officer. He talked to the officer who had refused me entry and waved me through. At least there was one policeman on duty with some commonsense.

We were sat near the front of the stand, so I could peer over the side to the empty terrace below. We were in the West Stand. This was the stand where some fans from pens 3 and 4 were rescued, as other fans pulled them up from that terrace up into the safety of the stand. Those thoughts flashed through my mind. I dropped the flowers into the empty terrace below, just like many other fans had done. The game started, but it didn't really matter. It was the occasion what really mattered and what it meant to those Liverpool fans present that night and the significance of it all. We lost the game 2 – 0 but it meant nothing. I'm sure the players were not really up for that game, at that venue. I am convinced that the enormity of it all was the reason why they did not perform that night. Everybody in that West Stand realised that – all except for one person – Edward. His cold, callous, uncaring nature came to the fore. He shouted a tirade of abuse at the Liverpool players at the end of the game, along the lines of 'useless,' 'inept' 'absolute rubbish.' How pathetic. He was the only one. I am not sure how, but nobody smacked him, not even me. I was too traumatised to care, but inside I was fuming. So were Sharon and Lynn. To care more about the result than the significance of what returning to Hillsborough for the first time since the disaster actually meant, really does smack of a poverty of feeling in my mind. I kept looking into that empty terrace and thinking about the 15th of April, as sadness glazed across my face. I just wanted a few minutes alone, to look down there and reflect and think. Nobody could deny me those few minutes.

I had got through the RETURN TO HELL. It wasn't a pleasant experience, it was never going to be. I have not been able to return there since, not in 23 years. I often thought will I ever go back? I have often had that feeling of wanting to 'retrace the steps' I took that fateful day at some point in the very near future. In recent times, I thought about it more. I have returned there. There is more about this later on.

Another league title was won, our 18th and the last up to now. Another season ticket was renewed. It would appear that everything was 'normal.' But in truth it wasn't. The 1990 – 1991 season was to be my last for quite a while. It just was not the same watching Liverpool, it never had been since Hillsborough. A part of me died that day, as well as my love for football. So much was taken from so many people.

The first game of the season meant a return to Sheffield. This time to Bramall Lane, the home of Sheffield United. A not very pleasant experience happened to me that day. The fact that we were in Sheffield some 18 months after the Hillsborough Disaster, brought it all back to me once more. It was a decent game, a 2 – 2 draw. The signs were there, however, that the current team was losing it's grip of dominance in the English game. In fact, the warning signs were there the season before. Although we won the league, it was probably the worst championship winning side in living memory. We had an ageing team, as well as replacements who were not of the quality that was required. The selling of John Aldridge was a big mistake. The 1990 FA Cup semi-final loss to Crystal Palace was further evidence that things were not right. This was the team, remember, who we trounced 9 – 0 earlier on in the season. This aside, it had been a good day out. I was walking back to the car, when I was confronted by this Sheffield neanderthal. I managed to walk away from a very explosive situation as a policeman approached. Did this complete moron not realise what we as Liverpool fans had been through in that city some 18 months earlier? I can guess that he was one of those Sheffield residents who blamed us for the disaster. My love for football was falling apart at the seams. It was not helped by idiots like the Sheffield United fan who was spoiling for a fight. Furthermore, I was struggling with PTSD. The nightmares and the flashbacks were getting worse. I was drinking more and pretending I was enjoying it, when in reality, I wasn't.

I started getting into watching top class Rugby Union shortly after Hillsborough. It was something different to football. The crowds in club and competitive league games were smaller than at football matches, but there was no police presence, no hooliganism, no segregation, no caged pens, no police escorts. You could happily stand and sit with opposing fans, enjoy a laugh and a few drinks, without the fear of being beaten to a pulp. This was a refreshing change. I had played Rugby in my younger days so I knew the game. I always used to enjoy watching the big international rugby occasions on the BBC at Twickenham, Cardiff Arms Park, Murrayfield, Lansdowne Road and The Park de Princes in the old Five Nations Championship (now the Six Nations since the introduction of Italy). So when some friends of mine moved down to Gloucester and invited me down for the weekend, I jumped at the chance. I was given a seat ticket for the old Grandstand at Kingsholm to watch Gloucester play Coventry in a club match. The club matches were gradually being phased out since the relatively new inception of a competitive league. However, they were still very 'tasty' affairs with brutal forward battles being contested. I thoroughly enjoyed the experience of my first visit to Kingsholm, the home of Gloucester RFC. A place very similar to Anfield in respect of the atmosphere and the most passionate fans in the game. Liverpool has The Kop, Gloucester has The Shed!!!

Of course a lot of drinking is done at Rugby matches. I guess in a way, watching Rugby did not help my battle with PTSD in relation to the amount of alcohol I consumed. But it became an obsession of mine for 20 years. I guess you could say that I was fighting this psychological battle by trying to forget Hillsborough, forget football, forget the lies, the fabrications, the cover ups. I was trying to forget about witnessing so much horrific death, and all the pain that went with that. I was trying to forget about Duckenfield and the whole bastard force that was South Yorkshire

Police. I was trying to forget about Popper and those blood-alcohol tests, the false accusations and the vile questioning in the gymnasium. I was trying to forget about those inquests, which were a complete sham, that put the families and the survivors, and indeed, those that died on trial. I was trying to forget about the twenty years of heartache, hurt and pain inflicted upon me because of Hillsborough. I was convincing myself that Rugby, coupled with huge amounts of alcohol, actually helped me. I have come to realise in the last few months that that is simply not the case. I was not facing my demons.

So, by the start of the 1991 – 1992 season, I had sent back my season ticket and got a full refund. I was totally finished with football. I think after Kenny Dalglish left that was the final straw for me. He pointed to illness as the primary reason for his resignation and the fact he was badly affected by Hillsborough. I was the same. If King Kenny could not take it anymore then neither could I.

The next few years were fuelled with drink, anger, frustration, PTSD, Rugby and very boozy holidays. I was given almost five thousand pounds in compensation because of Hillsborough, which I pissed against the wall, for the use of a better phrase. My life was in a sad state of affairs. I was this very different person who used anger as a tool to get by in life. I was terrible towards my family, especially my loving parents. I was very abusive and confrontational towards them. I also withdrew into an introverted shell, whereas before I had been much more open and at times, extroverted. I am not trying to pass the blame here, but PTSD and my experiences of Hillsborough contributed greatly to the person I became. But in November 1994 something would happen that would shatter my life and that of my family to it's very core. The death of my brother Anthony......

Chapter Nine

Anthony: YNWA

Anthony Whittle was born on the 3rd of November 1964. He was my younger brother. We often fought like cat and dog, as brothers often do. But deep down, I know we loved and cared for each other. I know he was genuinely worried when I was at Hillsborough. Anthony, if truth be told, did not have a very happy adult life. He started suffering from depression in his teenage years when he was taking his GCSE's. This developed into adult life into a severe mental illness, where he suffered nervous breakdowns and in the end Paranoid Schizophrenia. A number of sour relationships and at times, a troubled marriage, did not help matters. Yet, for a time, it seemed that he was a lot happier in his life.

I know that he tried to take his own life when he was about 20 years of age. I would not want to go too deeply into the case, but I know that Anthony had been drinking and he took a hose pipe from the garage and borrowed my Dad's car. He attempted to intoxicate himself with exhaust fumes. He was in a very sorry, desperate state. Anthony had also threatened someone at a house up on the moors. He was not thinking straight, obviously. He had a long stick, which he thought was a gun. Eventually, the police were called and he was arrested. I didn't go to the police station, but my Dad did. Anthony was in such a sorry, pitiful state. The police, who were far from sympathetic, a familiar story, insisted that they would press charges unless he was sectioned under the Mental Health Act. So Anthony ended up at the psychiatric unit at Burnley General Hospital. When we went to visit him we found he was drugged up to the eyeballs, wandering round the ward like a zombie. I must say that the care he received through Burnley Mental Health Services was quite appalling. He was virtually left to fend for himself. We were not having this, so we went to see our GP. He was not much use either. After insulting my Mother and questioning if it was time for her appointment, Dr. Smith was less than sympathetic. After much arm twisting he agreed to contact Airedale General Hospital, over the border in Yorkshire. We were given an appointment for Anthony with the psychiatric services there. What we found was a totally different attitude and treatment. They were absolutely fantastic with us, and more importantly, with Anthony. We managed to get him a place in the psychiatric unit, from which he really benefited. The consultant psychiatrist insisted that the best way for treatment was not to be given an almost limitless supply of drugs, but to take part in all activities, exercising your mind and body, which brought about a positive affect. Anthony could not want for anything at Airedale. They had a gymnasium and sports facilities and were encouraged to use these facilities as much as possible. They were given tests to encourage using their brains and to 'feed their minds' as much as possible. They were also expected to do daily chores such as washing up and making their own beds. They also had to make themselves look presentable. There was no 'feeling sorry for themselves' or doing absolutely nothing. It was a strict regime of hard work, exercise and healthy eating. And it worked.

When Anthony was allowed home for the weekend after a few weeks 'proving himself,' he was a different person. Eventually, he was released after a few short months and decided that he would take a trip around Europe. He was given some medication by the hospital that he needed to take regularly. I recall that we received a postcard from Anthony whilst he was in Salou. He seemed to be at peace with himself and the world.

As the years rolled on, so his health slowly deteriorated. He got married in 1991. I don't have much contact with his widow, but I do with his stepson, David, my nephew. I took it on board to be like a father figure to him after Anthony died. As it happens, David has turned out quite well. The marriage did have a few problems along the way, but I won't go into that. I want to focus on his last remaining days and weeks. When his death came it was not expected, and to be honest it floored us.

To his credit, Anthony tried to better himself by going to college and gaining new qualifications. In turn, he applied for university to study Forestry. He was accepted to study a degree course at the University of Wales, in Bangor. We were immensely proud of him. My parents showed it more than I did. After all, PTSD had firmly grabbed control of my life. But deep down inside, I was really proud of him. Initially, Anthony seemed to settle in very well in Bangor, where he was housed in student accommodation. He made a few new friends with other students on his course. At first, he managed to cope with the workload of the course quite well. He looked forward to developing a career in this field. The first time that we felt concerned that things might not be quite right with Anthony was a couple of weeks before his death. He said that he might come home for the weekend, although this never materialised. He then rang home quite regularly and said that the work was getting him down. A few days before he died he said he wanted to come home and that he had been experiencing nightmares. He got to ringing a few times a day. On his last telephone call he said he would travel up to Chester by train. So it was decided that me and my Dad should drive down to Chester to meet him and my Mum would wait by the telephone. So we set off early in the morning, and drove down to Chester. It was the 24th of November, my Mum's birthday. When we arrived at Chester railway station there was no sign of him. We waited in case he was on another train. Nothing. I rang home and told my Mum. It was decided that we should drive down to Bangor. We drove down the A55 North Wales coast road, which has stunning scenery. Yet, that scenery did not concern us. What did concern us was Anthony's health, his mental state and his well-being. When we arrived in Bangor we headed straight for the university. We telephoned home to tell my Mum that we had arrived in Bangor and we were going to try to locate Anthony. We drove up to the university before being directed to the halls of residence. Once we were there he checked out his room. There was some scribbled writing, which talked about the 'devil coming to get him.' My Dad managed to chat to one of his fellow students who said he had headed home. We then took some of his belongings and headed into Bangor where we would ring home once more.

My Mum had received a call from Llandudno police, who told her that Anthony had been picked up on Llandudno beach wearing only one shoe. He apparently was in a 'terrible state.' Naturally, she was very worried so we headed straight for Llandudno. Once we had found the police station, my Dad went inside to talk to them and to try to get Anthony released into our care. We were too late, by five minutes. He had been taken to a secure mental health unit in Bangor, called The Hergest Unit. We had to drive back to Bangor, yet again.

When we arrived at The Hergest Unit, we hurriedly went over to the entrance and we were let in. It was a new, modern building. We were asked to wait until Anthony was brought to us in this small lounge. He seemed so quiet, withdrawn. He wanted to go home. He hugged us both, and said that he 'had changed.' We weren't bothered about that, all we cared about was that he was safe. It was the last time we would see him alive. Anthony was taken to a private room, as the doctor wished to speak with us alone. We explained to the doctor – his name was Dr. McGonagle – that we wished to take him home. He said that we couldn't, as they wanted to evaluate him. With that we sat in the waiting area, very tired and hungry. Within a few short minutes we heard a lot of noise from one of the private rooms. The staff just sat there initially, drinking tea. After a few minutes we found out that Anthony had escaped from his room and got outside. It was supposed to be a secure unit, yet he managed to escape. We always blamed McGonagle and the staff for what happened to Anthony. As we saw it, if they had been doing their jobs then he would have not got out of that unit. We were offered a bed in that unit for the night, just in case Anthony was found. We set off back home early the following morning. I had an awful feeling in the pit of my stomach as we drove back. My Dad was in tears. I think he knew deep down something had happened to him.

When we arrived back home my Mum told me of the contact she had with Burnley police. How they were far from respectful with our situation. As you can imagine, the police were not my favourite people at that time, not after what happened at Hillsborough and how it controlled my life. My Dad went to bed to try and get some sleep and my Mum nipped out to the local shop. I was just sat there on my own. I was thinking the worst, you always do in scenarios like that. You always dread such moments, the walk down your path, the knock on the door, and it happened in those few minutes when I was alone. A police car pulled up and out climbed a uniformed officer. Was he really coming to our house? He was. The moment just knocks you down flat as if you have been punched square on the jaw by a world champion heavyweight boxer. Anthony was missing and a policeman pays you a visit. It is obviously not going to be good news. You dread and fear about such moments. I have never been able to get my head round the moment when I looked out of the window in our front room and my Mum saw the policeman there. I saw her heart sink to her knees. By this time I had dragged my Dad out of bed frantically telling him, "Dad, Dad, the police are here." As my Mum and Dad sat in the living room, I stood up, facing the police constable. He was only young, and I often wondered if he had ever had to do this task before in his career.

"Have they found him? Have they found Anthony?" I asked nervously.

"Sort of," was the reply. "His body was found this morning. It appears he has taken his own life."

The news just knocked us completely. The intense shock sent our emotions reeling. We all just wept openly, uncontrollably. I hugged my Mum and Dad close, something that I hadn't been able to do since before Hillsborough. The policeman left us to our grief, saying that he was deeply sorry. It must have been hard for this young PC to tell us that Anthony was dead. However, he certainly should not have said that 'he appears to have taken his own life.' This was not fact, it was merely hear say and an opinion based on his mental state and where his body was found. He should only have said that if he had indisputable proof. Obviously, we were distraught. I had been hit with two massive tragedies in five years. A double whammy you might say. How would I cope? One thing is for certain, I had to cope for my parents sake. They needed me more than ever now.

The next few days were chaotic to say the least. Not only had we to deal with grief and the tragic event of Anthony's death, we also had the awful task of telephoning relatives and friends to tell them the tragic news. Yet, some found out via the media. Another organisation that I have little time for. Some relatives found out of Anthony's death on local radio. A radio station by the name of Red Rose Radio gave it out on air and all the gory details. We contacted the radio station and they denied any knowledge of the report going out on air. We contacted our solicitor who in turn discussed matters with management at the radio station. Our solicitor pointed out to them that they would have a tape recording on the report. It later transpired that the tape 'could not be found' or 'did not exist.' Does it sound familiar? I cannot help but think back to Hillsborough and the 'missing tapes' in the police control room. Another cover up. Not only that, we also had the press hounding us for stories and had to read some of the crap in newspapers, which were inaccurate to say the least. I do not know where they got the stories from, it certainly was not from us. I would not like to divulge too much about those press reports as they are personal and they hurt myself and my family very deeply. However, I will use one example. A local newspaper claimed that Anthony 'charged about like a frightened animal before jumping to his death.' How did they know this? Nobody saw him outside after he escaped from The Hergest Unit. After all, it was a cold, dark night in late November. It was crass, sensationalist reporting of the lowest kind. And how do they know that he jumped to his death? They had no undeniable proof of this.

I had to take time off the training course I was on. I was given as long as I wanted. The funeral had to be arranged, the body identified, a post mortem carried out. The body was identified by Dr. McGonagle as that of Anthony. The post mortem carried out stated that he died from injuries sustained from a drop from a great height, namely a road bridge in Bangor, North Wales. The head injuries were the primary cause of death and his back was broken. The funeral was arranged for the following week and the parish priest from Saint John the Baptist Roman Catholic Church, Burnley, came to visit us in our home. His name was Father Leo Heakin, he was truly wonderful to us in our time of need. There was something that was carrying me through this intensely difficult time. My parents have often described that what I did during that period in their life which was earth shattering and beyond reason as me being like 'a rock.' It had to be done. After all, I would do anything for my brother, Anthony.

ANTHONY WHITTLE
3rd NOVEMBER 1964 – 25TH NOVEMBER 1994
REST IN PEACE.

Chapter Ten

Faith, Hope & Love

Immediately after Anthony's death, I felt something which is very hard to explain. It was a kind of guidance, like I was being 'cared for.' I truly know what it was and is now, my faith was renewed the day that Anthony died. I was being rescued and protected by God, Our Lord Jesus Christ, the Holy Spirit. Those non-believers that read this might scoff and mock. Yet, those who possess a strong faith or, indeed, have been reborn in Christ, will have some understanding of what happened to me. This was, after all, my darkest hour. I had just lost my younger brother, my terrible battle with PTSD was at it's worst, and five years earlier I had been at Hillsborough. I really could not have gone any lower. I actually think I felt something was there on that journey back from Bangor.

On the day that Father Leo Heakin visited us to arrange the funeral mass, which was to be a full requiem, I had this sudden urge to return to church. I had not been a regular attender for some 17 years. I told Father Leo this. He immediately gave me general absolution from all of my sins. It felt to be such a wonderfully uplifting moment. I returned to church the following Sunday, a few days before the funeral. It was a difficult thing to do but it is something I needed to accomplish. I felt very nervous walking through those church doors for the first time in years, but I have done so virtually every week since. I think walking through those doors, and ultimately Anthony's death, actually saved my life. I know for a fact that if I had not renewed my faith, gone back to church, I would not be around writing this account today. I am not saying it was an instant cure of all my ills, it certainly was not. I still have had times when things have been far from good. There have been times when PTSD has haunted me and basically made me feel like crap. There have been times when heavy drinking has still controlled my life. Yet, I regard it as a slow healing process where I have gradually recovered from the absolute hell I was in. The spiritual strength from faith is a great healer, as is the power of prayer. It is the best medication in the world and it is absolutely free!!!

I still had to get through the trauma of Anthony's funeral. The days following his death, I was totally reliant on alcohol to get me through, certainly to get me to sleep. The day of the funeral, I was determined to stay sober for his sake at least. His friends brought a huge floral tribute to the house, flowers made up in the word of 'TONY.' It was a nice gesture. What I could not cope with was arriving at church in the funeral cortege and the appearance that people just looking at you. The paranoia was setting in. The PTSD coming to the fore. I know everyone was there, paying their last respects and to honour Anthony's life, but, in my mind at least, I could not face them looking at me. Why were they staring? Were they blaming me? I really wanted to get out of that car and confront them. I was, however, too choked up in grief and emotion to do anything. I had to get through this day. I had to get my parents through it, more importantly.

The requiem mass was a very sad, sombre, yet prayerful occasion. The church was packed with family, friends and members of the parish. Father Leo led a wonderful service and several people had come up from the university to pay their respects, tutors and students alike. Like my Dad had tearfully said, 'I am determined that we will give him a good send off.' It had to be said that was the case. There were a lot of floral tributes, a lot of mass and sympathy cards. I do believe that Anthony touched a lot of peoples lives. After the requiem, it was like we had to go through it all again for the short service at the Cremaetorium. I would have preferred a Christian burial, but Anthony never did, according to his wife. He was cremated after a short service conducted by Father Leo Heakin. A favourite song which Anthony liked was played – 'On Your Shore' by Enya.

We came back to the house for refreshments. All our family and friends were there as well as those from university who had a long journey back to Wales. I felt very uncomfortable around everyone. I was disappearing into the shell of paranoia and low self esteem which had afflicted me since Hillsborough. I still had this notion that everyone was staring at me, I felt especially so around those from the university. I just wanted the day to end. I wanted to grieve alone. I wanted to get my parents through this hell. I just had to get out of the house. Later on, when most of the guests had left, I drove the few miles to the training centre with my nephew, David as company. Those at the centre were surprised to see me. I told my tutor that I wanted to return to the course the following week. I needed to get back into a routine, bury myself in work and take my mind away from the whole sorry episode. As I have learnt over the years, bereavement is a slow process and you do just take one day at a time. It is also true what many people say who have been profoundly affected by death and grief – 'You never get over it, you just learn to accept it.'

You also know who your friends are at times like these. I had kept in touch with Sharon, Lynn and Edward, even though I didn't go to the games anymore. I was in tears when I told Lynn Taylor and Sharon Crabtree about Anthony. I asked them if they would come to the funeral. Sharon couldn't come because she couldn't get time off work, but Lynn said she would, as she was not working at the time. She never came. I cut the pair of them off completely and they never contacted me for over four years. I sensed a deep feeling of guilt on their part because of what transpired. Edward stayed away for a few weeks to 'give us time as a family.' To his credit, he regularly visited us and kept in touch.

That Christmas was not a very happy one, being only a few short weeks after Anthony's death. But we had to get through it and treat things as 'normal' as possible, for David's sake. I drank heavily through most of Christmas and New Year. When 1995 came, we had something else to face – the inquest into Anthony's death and whether or not we would proceed with a civil case against The Hergest Unit and Dr. McGonagle. I really did not have the stomach for a fight in the courts. I know that might sound very defeatist, some might say gutless, a classic sign of weakness, or even horrible, but it was a fact. I knew, after Hillsborough, how those in authority, always get away with it, things get covered up, everything is swept under the carpet. I couldn't even face going to the inquest, which was held in Bangor. My Dad went with our solicitor. I didn't trust anyone in looking after my late brother's interests. I had a very bad anxiety attack that day. I was worried that there might be a car crash and my Dad might get killed. Ever since Hillsborough, I have had this deep fear and intense anxiety, thinking that something would happen to my loved ones, something so tragic, so awful, that I just would not be able to cope with it all. Nothing did happen, but that is what PTSD does to you.

When my Dad returned from Bangor, he gave us the verdict of the inquest. There were three possible outcomes – unlawful killing, accidental death or misadventure/suicide. We were convinced that Anthony did not take his own life, despite his severe mental state. We thought that unlawful killing through negligence by the hospital would be a verdict, which was possible but most unlikely. Our solicitor advised us that the most likely outcome would be either accidental death or misadventure/ suicide. We fervently hoped and prayed it would not be a suicide verdict. Anything but that. My Dad was fairly shaken by what he had witnessed in the coroner's court. All the details were particularly graphic and pulled no punches. I really should have gone and supported him, I know that now. But I had seen and heard enough about death to last a hundred or more lifetimes. I just could not face that inquest. The court listened to the evidence submitted and took the testimonies of the pathologist, who stated that in his opinion the injuries were 'consistent with a fall from a height and the way he fell and indeed landed pointed clearly to an accident. It did not appear, therefore, that suicide played a part in Mr. Whittle's death.'

The coroner listened to testimonies given by hospital staff, who maintained that a strong male of that age could easily break out of the unit. This was despite the fact that the Hergest Unit was meant to be secure. They felt that there was no negligence on their part, even though staff sat around drinking cups of tea whilst Anthony broke out of that unit. The doctor on duty that night, Dr. McGonagle, stated that he was deeply affected by Anthony's death and that he had the none too pleasant task of identifying the body to 'save the family any more grief or trauma.' How very commendable. Yet, we were blamed for not joining in the search for Anthony when he finally announced that he had escaped from that secure unit. We were emotionally and physically tired after such a long day of driving up and down the country, as well as being traumatised. We also did not know the area, so how the hell were we supposed to search for him? Another case of passing the blame, sweeping things under the carpet, covering up – just like Hillsborough.

The coroner gave the verdict of 'accidental death.' It was not the verdict that we really wanted. Yet, it was not the verdict, which we genuinely feared we would get either. There was some comfort that Anthony did not take his own life. The next stage in the process was whether or not we should carry on with legal proceedings against the Hergest Unit and Dr. McGonagle. The solicitor warned us it would be a difficult case to prove and could be expensive, meaning that we would have to apply for legal aid. As it transpired, we could not take the case any further as legal aid was not granted. Another case of not getting any justice for our loved one – just like at Hillsborough.

It was a case of trying to get my life back on track, following the inquest. At least now we could, as a family, grieve properly. It hit my Mum and Dad hard. After all, you don't expect as parents to lose your son. They were both pensioners – my Dad was 75, my Mum being 68. They needed me, meaning I dismissed my own health issues to support them. I couldn't grieve as they could. I couldn't show what I felt inside. I bottled it all up again, just like I did following Hillsborough. They described me as their 'rock.' I didn't feel like their rock, far from it. How did I cope? In truth, I didn't. The only thing that kept me going was my faith. Going to church was a huge blessing for me. It was the one thing that kept me going when everything seemed to be rock bottom in my life. It was the one glint of light inside that very dark tunnel. Yes, I still drank heavily. Yes, I still had deep rooted problems with PTSD. But my faith was there if I needed it to get me through the low points in my life.

My Dad became ill towards the end of 1996. He was losing weight and looked pale and grey. We first noticed this in August, whilst we were on holiday in Cornwall. He had lost his appetite and was not eating as he normally would. The holiday was the last that we would have at the guest house where we had stayed many times over the years since 1983. It was run by Jim and Elsie Mercer, who had become good friends with us all. They lived in the beautiful Cornish village of Downderry, some 12 miles south of Plymouth. Their house, Eddystone Cottage, overlooked the sea, and was just a short walk to the beach. It was heaven. Sadly, Jim and Elsie were selling up and were moving back up north to Lancashire. We had a good holiday, but were increasingly concerned by my Dad's health.

As winter approached, my Dad was getting worse. One Sunday morning, whilst I was at Mass, he collapsed and was rushed into hospital. When I got to hospital, he passed out a number of times in A & E. A doctor told us that there might be a tumor, but that they had caught it early. My Dad was moved to a ward and tests were done. He was operated on the next day. A tumor was removed from his bowel and the consultant said the rest of his bowels were clear. The relief that my Mum and I felt was overwhelming. He had cancer, but it had been caught early. I am convinced, even today, that the cancer was caused directly by the loss of Anthony. My Dad spent about 10 days in hospital, but was sent home before Christmas. It was a Christmas that I could enjoy to a certain extent. However, it was the third Christmas without Anthony, and he was still deeply missed. But you learn to cope with grief over the passage of time, and the fact that my Dad had survived cancer was a blessing and brought about much needed joy and relief in our home.

As the years rolled by, so my faith grew stronger. The PTSD was still there, the heavy drinking continued, though to a lesser extent. The slow healing process had begun. I was in it for the long haul, I had to be. When you are emotionally damaged goods like I am, you have to be prepared for the long process of healing and recovery. My faith helped that process and it was the main reason for my healing. I know that my Mum was really proud when I decided that I wanted to return to the church. It was something which I just had to do. I look back now, and it is probably the best decision I have made in my entire life. It was a focus point.

I still missed going to watch Liverpool. My biggest regret was not going for 'The Kop's Last Stand' against Norwich City on the 1st of May 1994, a few short months before Anthony's death. Yet, such was the state of my mind, and the seriousness of my illness, I just could not even contemplate going to that game, which will be forever etched on the memories of Liverpool fans all over the world, not so much the game which Liverpool lost 1 – 0, but with what the occasion signified, the end of the standing Kop at Anfield. I had stood on The Kop for years, many as a season ticket holder, a true Kopite. But I could not go to this emotionally charged occasion. However, my love for Liverpool never died, nor never waned. I spent something like eight years not going to Anfield to watch my beloved Liverpool. Yet, the desire was always there. A deep, burning Red fire in my heart. It was inevitable, therefore, that I should want to return at some stage. This return coincided with an increased sense of my own faith. The church, in scripture, often talks about forgiveness. In The Lords Prayer, it mentions forgiveness – 'Forgive us Lord our trespasses, as we forgive those who trespass against us.' As I felt this spiritual strength, I wanted to return to watching Liverpool. Something drew me back towards Anfield. I also felt I had to write to Sharon and Lynn. I had spent nearly five years not talking to them, which was stupid and uncalled for. I had to forgive them for not being there for me when Anthony died. After all, life is too short. They rang me and we settled our differences. So in August 1999, I was back at Anfield for the first time in eight years. The first game, a rather disappointing 1 – 0 defeat to Watford. Still, it was great to be back 'home.' We went on the train that day, getting off at Kirkdale station. Old memories. Old friends.

I attended as many home games as I could get tickets for up to September 2001. In fact I only missed a handful of games at Anfield during that period. It was really fantastic to be back. During that time, Sharon passed her driving test and bought a car. So we travelled together getting there early doors. We often enjoyed a meal together with wine or beer or both in my case once we got back from the match. Everything seemed fine and I was at peace with the world. It was better to travel in Sharon's car than with Edward, which we did before she passed her test. We usually only got there about an hour or so before kick off so it did not leave much time for libations in The Albert!!! At least with Sharon you were able to make more of a day of it.

There was one occasion which I can recall, when I was drinking a bottle of lager in the back of the car and I spilt it all over the seat. We made a laugh and a joke about it and I am pretty sure that I apologised. It was towards the end of the season. I thought nothing more of it. A few short weeks later, she had her car vandalised and it was burnt out by some low life hooligans. Thankfully, it was in the close season. We kept in touch over the summer and she eventually purchased a new car. Everything seemed set for the new season. I was looking forward to it immensely. After all, Liverpool had just won a treble of cups the previous season, under Gerard Houllier – UEFA Cup, FA Cup and League Cup. It must be said that optimism was sky high. I had been friends with Sharon and Lynn for a long time, since the early 1980's when we travelled by train. I naturally thought that everything would be as normal for the forthcoming season. A journey to Anfield by car, a good laugh, banter, songs and arriving in plenty of time. The ideal scenario. Unfortunately, it did not quite work out that way. I contacted Sharon by email, as a game was coming up. I needed to sort out arrangements to be picked up. I tried to make my email humorous, along the lines of 'Am I going to end up going with that baldy old fart' relating to Edward. I know it was cruel and maybe I should not have said that. Yet, they themselves had constantly made jokes at Edward's expense, recalling his tight-fisted and rather boring nature over many years. I got a reply from Sharon. The email was quite terse in it's manner. I was told 'Look Chris, I cannot take you anymore. There are two guys from work who have season tickets and I am taking them instead.' What? I was totally shocked by the response. Did our friendship not count for anything? Did what we went through at Hillsborough mean absolutely nothing? Why do such a thing? Maybe, thinking back, it was to do with the spilt bottle of lager in the car. I just did not get a straight answer. We have not spoken since that day, something like eleven years ago. What was pathetic was that at Christmas of that year, they (Sharon and Lynn) sent a Christmas card to my Mum and Dad, without my name on it. I have come to realise that they were never true friends. I arranged with Edward to take me to the game. When he arrived at my home, he mentioned 'the email.' Sharon had actually told him what I had said in that email. I was told that there would be 'no drinking in the car, and it was straight back after the match, no quick pint in the pub.' I was so wound up. I went with him to the match. We never spoke a word going or coming back. He hurriedly walked off and left me as he locked the car. I know that I should not have said what I did in that email, but the behaviour of all three of them was sadly pathetic. It was the last match that I went to for quite a while. I could not afford the train travel, and I did not have a car at that time. Another issue was the fact that I was having recurring problems with PTSD at that time. I could not cope again.

As bad as my PTSD was, I found solace through my faith. The previous September I had gone back to college to study a course in Bereavement. I wrote an essay on Hillsborough, in which the tutor complemented me for my work. There was talk of a bereavement group being set up at church. It was something which interested me, given my experiences. I thought that it could end up being a positive in my life. I also signed up for another couple of courses at college in September 2001. I needed something to occupy my mind. I studied Psychology and a course entitled 'Understanding and Supporting Clients Needs' which was also Psychology based. Going back to college was absolutely brilliant for me. It gave my low self esteem a real shot in the arm. By this time, I was very much actively involved in church life. I was part of the team which ran the 'Journey in Faith' programme, in which adults learnt more about Christianity through the ALPHA course, which ran up to Christmas. In the New Year everything focused on teachings, scripture and sacraments of the Roman Catholic faith. At Easter, any new members would be welcomed into the Catholic Church. It really was uplifting for me and my faith grew because of it. I actually delivered a talk each year on the 'Journey in Faith' programme. This was entitled 'Death of a Christian' and told of my Hillsborough experiences, the loss of my brother, Anthony and my subsequent return to the church. I was praised by many people regarding the talk over a number of years.

I was part of other ministries as well, such as the Welcoming Ministry, where I would welcome worshippers into church for Mass with a smile and a friendly word or two. I am still involved in this today, at Mass every Sunday morning. I have also done church work for CAFOD (Catholic Aid For Overseas Development) as well as being involved with SPUC (Society for the Protection of Unborn Children) in which I produced and edited a quarterly magazine. I have been active in the development of children within church life through the Sacramental Programme, in which they are taught about the sacraments and church life. What is most special, however, regarding the work that I have done within the church is the role of a Eucharistic Minister, which I have done for about 10 years now. It is a very special, yet humbling honour to serve Our Lord on the altar. It is something which I value and cherish greatly. It fills me with pride and a burning desire to serve God.

At this point in my life, I felt something was taking shape and I was developing as a person. Everything was not perfect, far from it. I still had major issues with PTSD, but my reliance on alcohol was not what it once was. I had decided to apply to go to university to study for a degree as a mature student. I know what you are saying, given my age and all that, a very mature student!!! It was something I felt that I would like to do and achieve something worthwhile. At the same time, I was doing another year on the 'Journey in Faith' programme at church. This turned out to be a very special year indeed!!! I was to meet my future wife on the programme. Deborah had recently returned to Burnley after getting divorced and joined the Journey in Faith programme, being encouraged to do so by her parents. I had known her parents for a number of years through church activities. I know it sounds cheesy but I was instantly attracted to Deborah. It took me a lot longer though to summon up the courage and ask her out!!!

There was just something about her that set Deborah apart from the other girls that I had dated. A very caring, loving nature, she will do anything for anybody. I needed reassurance, as well as that intense love thing. I needed a soulmate, a shoulder to cry on, a rock that I could head for in the stormy sea that was my very complicated life. That was, and is, Deborah. I did not just take on Deborah in the summer of 2002, I took on a ready made family in the form of her two children, Zachary and Kendra. This was to be a challenge that would test me, but one which has ultimately made me a better person and in the end brought a calming influence on my life.

I always wanted to have children but it never happened for me. I came on the scene just when I was preparing to go to university to study towards a degree. I cannot say life was easy with my new family, in fact there were difficult times ahead. I carried a lot of excess baggage, most notably with PTSD. There was also the added stress of studying at university. From the outset, Kendra and I clashed many times. There was fault on both sides. I did not fully understand what it was like to be a stepparent and readjustment was needed. I guess I did not fully understand Kendra at that time. On the other side of the coin, I felt that Kendra did not give me the respect that I deserved, and that her mouth often got her in trouble. We were both wrong, but I guess I failed at times to fully understand the terrible times she had gone through at such a young age. It was not just about my problems, so I guess you can say that I was being selfish. Kendra was only 11 when I came on the scene and she had certain issues which I will not divulge as that is a private family matter. However, the divorce of her parents rocked her world and you could say that she had a deep mistrust of men. Gradually, over time, a much better relationship has developed between us. I believe now that our relationship is the best that it has ever been, and there is very little friction between us now. It is true to say that intelligence and knowledge is gained over a lifetime. You never stop learning and that is certainly true in my case.

Zachary is a different case altogether. He has had to cope with a form of autism for most of his life. He has Asperger's Syndrome, as well as motor control problems and dypraxia. He tends to like his own space and could be described as being a bit of an 'hermit.' Yet, he has done well in life, through study and work and has a dry sense of humour – not as funny as me, but pretty humourous nonetheless. He now, at age 24, holds down a regular job, which he has done so for several years. If he has a fault I would say that he can be deeply unmoralistic and at times arrogant, thinking he knows everything. However, he is certainly making a success of his life despite the obstacles put in his way.

My wife, Deborah, is a senior nurse at a BUPA care home, looking after residents with end stage dementia. It is a job that I simply could not do, yet she does it in such a fantastic way, with patience, understanding and great resolve. I know it is stressful for her, but she copes magnificently. It is the type of person she is – after all, she has to put up with me and the PTSD which still affects me from time to time. Deborah really is one in a million!!!

When I hit my 40's I thought 'Oh well, I don't think that I will ever marry.' I had just about given up hope. I actually prayed that I would meet the right person, after all, I had made some terrible choices as regards the opposite sex other the years. I really am blessed with this wonderful faith of mine. It really has helped me overcome problems and bring renewed hope into my life, at very difficult and troubled times. I often mention this, but the power of prayer is a wonderful 'medication' and it is free!!! I met Deborah in September 2001, at a time when life was not at it's best as regards PTSD. I was still studying at college, but no longer attended football games. I was committed to the Journey in Faith programme at church on Tuesday evenings, and that is where I first met Deborah. I had known her parents for several years through the programme. I gradually got to know Deborah, and was attracted to her immensely. I thought that this might be the one. However, it took me several months to pluck up enough courage to actually ask her out. It happens a lot to us men that!!! I was encouraged by a wonderful lady on the Journey in Faith programme, Helen Dolan. I had helped her to run a previous programme on Saturday mornings for children, so we had become good friends. Sadly, Helen died several years ago through cancer. She is much missed by the whole parish. Eventually, the following March, at Easter, I summoned up just enough courage to ask her out. Deborah had recently got divorced, so it was a massive step for her to take. After a brief time dating, Deborah broke it off. She could not handle a relationship, she was not ready to get involved romantically again. It rocked my world. It was the same night that Liverpool were playing in Europe, and losing to Bayer Leverkausen. I withdrew into my dark shell once more.

The months were long, slow and painful. We kept in touch and were still friends. In June, we celebrated my birthday. I was 41. We went for a meal and a few drinks at the 110 Club, a local catholic club in town. We decided to meet the following weekend and go up to Towneley Hall. Deborah invited me back to her place for a takeaway with herself and her two kids. This was the night that we fell in love and we have been together ever since, something like ten years.

With us both being catholic it was clear that we could not marry, as Deborah had previously been married in the church, the very church where we worshipped. The only way that we could marry was if the church granted an annulment to the marriage, and that was a long process. Yet, we were both prepared to go through with it. It truly was a difficult time, especially for Deborah, who had to go through the hell of recollecting what she had endured in her marriage, in meetings with the parish priest. I had to meet with him as well, but for Deborah it was far worse. I really deeply thank her for what she went through for me. It was a long process, going on towards two years. It was a nervous time for both of us, what if the annulment was not granted? What could we possibly do? I had every faith that it would be granted. The word 'faith' is a prominent one. My own faith grew stronger day by day. I felt that Our Lord helped me through this latest difficult time. I was doing well at university, and I was in love with Deborah. The next stage was that we were granted an annulment. It came in 2004, and we were engaged at Christmas of that year – the best Christmas ever!!! It truly was a wonderful time. I was in my final year at university, an annulment had been granted by the church, and Deborah and I were engaged. We arranged an engagement party on Boxing Day and the whole family – my side and Deborah's side attended.

The wedding was planned for May 2006. I had a tough year to get through, my final year at university and a dissertation to write, so it was felt that we should wait a good 18 months before we married, time enough to save up and plan things perfectly. The day, the most special day in the whole of my life, could not come soon enough. I often thought about walking down that aisle, on such a proud, happy, memorable occasion. I often thought back to 1994, and the sadness of Anthony's Requiem Mass in the very same church. The next time would be different. It would be my wedding day, and our Anthony would be looking down on me from above. As time passed, I got through my studies and obtained a Combined Honours degree in Education Studies with History from the University of Central Lancashire in 2005. Another case of getting my life back on track after years of hurt, anger and turmoil with PTSD.

The big day finally arrived – Saturday the 20th of May 2006. Our wedding day. We were to be married at Saint John the Baptist Roman Catholic Church, Burnley. The full Nuptial Mass was conducted by Father Michael Waters, the parish priest, and Father Simon Firth, the assistant priest. It was a truly wonderful occasion. My nephew, David, was best man, and chief bridesmaid was Kendra, my stepdaughter, well I should really say our daughter. The reception was held at the Alexander Hotel in Burnley (which is now closed, sad to say) and it really was a fantastically, happy day.

My whole life is fitting together perfectly. Everything, on the whole, now seems positive, and I have a lot to be thankful to God for. Yes, I still have PTSD issues at times, but my drinking is under control, my faith is strong, I have a loving family. What more could I ask for?

Chapter Eleven

Return to Hell

I recently made a return trip to Hillsborough, for the first time since November 1989, or should I say, a RETURN TO HELL. Here is my account of the day.

On Tuesday, 28ᵗʰ June 2011, together with my wife, Deborah, I returned to Sheffield, and to Hillsborough. It is something which I had been thinking about for a while, something which I could not have even contemplated doing for many years, but the time felt right to make that journey. I had to retrace the footsteps of the 15ᵗʰ of April 1989, I had to face my very own demons.

We set off to Sheffield by train, at 6:30am. We were to change at Leeds. It was a beautifully warm, sunny morning, pretty much like the 15ᵗʰ of April 1989. The journey was quiet and peaceful, and we had egg and bacon butties for breakfast, with steaming hot coffee. Once we got on the Leeds – Sheffield train, the more I started thinking deeply about Hillsborough. I had a churned up feeling in the pit of my stomach, there was intense trepidation, there was deep fear. As we got ever closer to Sheffield, I could not get the Manic Street Preachers song, 'SOUTH YORKSHIRE MASS MURDERERS' out of my head. Finally, we arrived in Sheffield, shortly before nine. I really could not describe my feelings at that moment. As we left the station, I noticed how different Sheffield was. After all, it was over 20 years since I was last there.

We headed for the tram stop at Queens Square. We took the tram to the Cathedral, and our first port of call – Sheffield Town Hall. This was where the sham of the main inquests were held, under the dubious jurisdiction of the corrupt coroner, Stefan Popper. We stayed here for about 10 minutes, and a police car drove up and down several times. Maybe I was being paranoid, but I actually thought that they were following me. Maybe they were. My wife and I then sat outside the Cathedral in quiet contemplation, before boarding another tram to Shalesmoor. We got off here in order to find the Sheffield Medico-Legal Centre, this is where the controversial mini-inquests were held, and some of the bodies were housed, where the bereaved, grief stricken relatives were treated disgracefully during the identification process. This red-bricked building looked cold, grey, inhospitable, callous, unwelcoming – pretty much like South Yorkshire Police and the coroner, Stefan Popper were, those 20 or more years ago. I bought some flowers and headed back to the tram stop – time to move on, to HELLSBOROUGH.

On the face of it, everything seemed so different. After all, it had been 23 years since I had been there. We got off the tram at Leppings Lane, right at the top, near to Hillsborough Primary School. This area was unfamiliar to me. We walked to the main entrance of Sheffield Wednesday Football Club, passing the almost insignificant memorial to the 96. Those brave souls, the 96 angels, certainly deserved a lot more than what that memorial signifies. I nervously went to reception and announced myself. A security man took us through to the pitch via the South Stand – a redeveloped Hillsborough Stadium. He commented on how things had changed since 1989. The security man, named Bob, was very respectful, and told us to take as long as we needed. We approached the old Leppings Lane End, and out of the corner of my eye, I noticed the police control box – the same police control box where Duckenfield screwed up, where Duckenfield lied to Graham Kelly, where Duckenfield caused the deaths of 96 people, where two video tapes with evidence of what happened were mysteriously 'stolen' on the night of the 15th of April 1989. I found a couple of seats close to where I was stood on that dreadful April afternoon 22 years ago. I lay the bunch of flowers on the floor, together with one of my poems – 'I CAME HOME.' There was an eerie feeling sat there, though I felt not to be alone. I have no doubt that the 96 angels were there with me. I honestly, truthfully, undoubtedly felt their presence – and that was a great, uplifting, wonderful comfort. They were looking after me. I got up and nervously approached the tunnel from the seated area – this is what I had been dreading the most. It was the same tunnel, with the same deep 6 in 1 gradient, but there was more light, not the one dim bulb that there was in 1989. The tunnel had also been painted. There was certainly less darkness there, but it was still the same tunnel of death. The walk back down the tunnel with it's steep gradient genuinely frightened me and it brought it all back, that sunny April afternoon as I descended the tunnel of death. I felt a shakiness, a deep fear, as if it was the 15th of April 1989 all over again. I returned to those seats with real fear. The inner concourse had the same horrible feel and ugly appearance about it, and it flashed across my mind that the only logical way, as it had been in 1989, was to go down the tunnel. As I looked back across towards the police control box, I could clearly see Bob, and Bob could clearly see me. It was plainly obvious that Duckenfield could clearly see what was going on in Pens 3 & 4, on that afternoon of the 15th of April 1989.

I asked Bob if we could leave via Leppings Lane. He agreed, and opened the large gate to let us out. I thanked him for escorting us and shook his hand. We walked out through the gate. To my horror, it was GATE C – the infamous Gate C. It was still there. As I walked along the outer concourse, I clearly noticed that some work has been done on that area and it is a little wider than it was in 1989. Still, nonetheless, it was a bottleneck. There are still railings by the river, but by Gate C, most of the large wall has been taken down. Yet. to me, nothing much has changed. As we walked along Leppings Lane, towards Penistone Road, everything still looked familiar – the street, the houses, the gardens. There has been some development as you turn into Penistone Road, and the telephone boxes seem to have gone. The two pubs, the Gate and the Travellers are both now closed. I noticed that the car park at the Travellers was fenced off. That is where we parked the car on the 15th of April 1989. It brought so many terrible, awful memories flooding back. We then walked up Penistone Road, towards Wadsley Bridge. There are two further pubs, the Bridge and the Railway, both of which are still open. There was a lot of building work going on, near to where we turned off in 1989, to be taken into the home of a kindly elderly couple. Rather than walk up Halifax Road, we decided to head back down the hill towards the corner shop, which many fans visited that day. Once past there, we walked on further towards the North Stand. We could clearly see that the club gymnasium was still there – the same gymnasium where many of those that died were held in body bags, with no dignity, where bereaved relatives were treated shamefully and interrogated with no thought, dignity or respect, where the rallying cry was 'the body belongs to the coroner now, not you.' An absolute disgrace, grief stricken relatives treated in the most callous, vicious and vile way, and where the coroner and South Yorkshire Police hatched their evil plot.

It had been a long and tiring day re-visiting Hillsborough. We headed back towards Leppings Lane, via a side street. I stared back at Gate C, unable to take it in that it actually was still there – more awful memories came flooding back, with me pinned against the wall near to that gate. I then stood by the river and looked down at the flowing water in quiet contemplation, thinking deeply about the 96, before we headed back to the tram stop to go back into Sheffield. I had managed to get through re-visiting Hillsborough.

We decided to go for a drink in honour of the 96. We found a nice little pub by the station called the Sheffield Tap. I thought about the day when I returned to Hillsborough. I thought about what happened to me over 23 years ago. I thought about the 96 angels and how I felt that they were there with me and how they guided me through this very difficult day. I thought about how I have finally managed to re-trace the steps of Hillsborough, and how I faced up to the fact that I actually had RETURNED TO HELL.

Chapter Twelve

At the End of the Storm
There's a Golden Sky

In this final chapter, I want to bring things right up to date, and how actually talking about Hillsborough to people like Anne Williams and others has helped me immensely. I am so proud to be associated with such wonderfully brave people as these. I have met a number of quite amazing people, and they are a credit to anyone who are involved in the continuing fight for justice. They are committed, brave, honourable, intelligent and unbowed. It is my pleasure to know them and had the opportunity to meet them. When I first got involved with HOPE FOR HILLSBOROUGH, I honestly did not have any idea where it would lead me. I had heard about Anne Williams, and had read her truly inspirational book. I finally got the chance to meet this remarkable lady recently and it was a truly wonderful, yet humbling experience. A great honour indeed.

I had often thought of doing some kind of fundraising activities, and after talking with Anne Williams, who was desperately trying to raise funds for her HOPE FOR HILLSBOROUGH group, it was decided that I should do a sponsored swim to raise as much money as I possibly could. I arranged with Pendle Wavelengths in Nelson to do the swim one Wednesday night in late September 2010. I was to do 50 lengths of the pool. I got the local media involved – the Lancashire Evening Telegraph and the Burnley Express – and sponsorship from many different people; friends, family, Liverpool fans, church parishioners et al. My wife, Deborah, came to support me, as well as fellow Liverpool fans from East Lancashire – Mick, Eric, Steve and John. Unfortunately, Anne Williams could not attend as she was poorly. I raised over £300 in total, which went to HOPE FOR HILLSBOROUGH. I was really proud of doing that swim, but my body ached for a few days afterwards!!!

In January 2011, I accompanied Anne Williams to London. She invited me along, as part of HFH, to meet with Jeremy Hunt MP, the Secretary of State for Culture, Media, the Olympics & Sport. Yes I did say HUNT!!! Mr. Hunt, following the World Cup in South Africa, made crass and vile comments regarding Hillsborough. His focus was meant to be on the success of the World Cup, and the fact that there had not been one England fan arrested during the tournament. This was an amazing achievement given the appalling record of the so-called England 'fans' over the years, in which they brought great shame to the country. Mr. Hunt, in a live TV interview, said:

"I think hooliganism is now a thing of the past. The problems that we had with Heysel and Hillsborough are now behind us."

What a totally crass and utterly stupid comment to make. It is FACT that Hillsborough was not down to hooliganism, but there is, unfortunately, a minority who still clings to that myth. Had Mr. Hunt researched Hillsborough thoroughly and properly, and had he got the true facts about the disaster, then I am sure he would not have made such a vile and uncalled for statement. Naturally, as a survivor, I was very angry when I heard those comments. An apology was demanded and received, but we at HFH wanted him to meet us and apologise face to face. He was urged to come to Liverpool and meet with us – he refused.

Instead, we had to go all the way down to London to meet him. This is typical of politicians. They are elected to help and serve the public, so it would be fair and proper for a government minister, who had made an awful blunder, to go out of his way to meet those very people that he had offended and upset. However, HFH acted with great dignity and respect, and we took the moral high ground, and decided to travel down to London by train to meet with Mr. Hunt. A Liverpool fan from London, Rupen Ganatra, kindly put us up for the night. We were to set off from Lime Street in the late morning. Anne Williams met me there, and she was interviewed by Granada Reports, a local ITV news programme. Unfortunately, a railway station employee, whose manner I could only describe as 'unfeeling' and 'arrogant' tried to stop the interview in an aggressive manner. I sincerely hope he never lost anyone at Hillsborough, or that he was a survivor. I suspect that with his attitude and lack of feeling that he had no connection to Hillsborough whatsoever.

Once we had boarded the train, we found our seats. Directly across from us was someone who was reading that lying gutter rag THE S*N. I wanted to snatch it from him and rip it up. There was deep anger on my face. Yet, I decided to take the moral high ground. It still hurts and cuts very deep inside of me, even today, what was written about me and my fellow Liverpool fans. All the lies, all the myths about drunken, ticketless yobs, of robbing from the dead, urinating on corpses, fighting with brave cops. What about the real, true picture of brave Liverpool fans, of selfless heroes, trying to save lives, or aid the injured and dying? It really does sicken me to my stomach.

As we travelled on the Virgin Pendolino to London, Anne discussed the case with me. She had a file at her disposal. We both spoke loud enough so that our S*N reader 'friend' could hear about all the lies, the injustice, the myths, the fabrications that was told, the cover ups, the false accusations, and the vile headlines in that gutter piece of filth that he was reading. I sincerely hope he felt uncomfortable and had a certain degree of guilt in his mind, in the sense that here was he reading that most odious of newspapers, and there we were talking about Hillsborough, and the biggest single miscarriage of justice in the history of the British legal system. Something which the S*n had played a significant part in.

When we arrived at London Euston, we were to meet with another survivor, Dean Harris, from South Wales. He was in Pen 4 that fateful day. We were also to meet a radio reporter, called Katie, from Real Radio, who was to cover the days events. Once we had all met, we adjourned for a coffee, before setting out by tube to Jeremy Hunt's offices near Trafalgar Square. It was a truly wet and horrible day in the capital, as we walked towards our destination. In Trafalgar Square, we met someone else who was to be at the meeting, Barrie Thompson, who had organised the March 4 Justice previously. Once we arrived at the offices we were asked to sign in and were giving visitors passes. We sat patiently in reception for our appointment. Anne noticed that two 'distinguished guests' for use of a better phrase were there. She told me that they were from the independent panel, set up by the previous government to look into Hillsborough. Anne had not been told that they would be there, and was therefore, rather dubious about their sudden appearance. There was the firm opinion between Anne and myself that they were there to 'keep an eye on us.'

We waited for a good ten or fifteen minutes before Jeremy Hunt met us and took us to a meeting room with a large table. We were offered refreshments of tea or coffee, and bottled water. I opted for water. We told our side of the story, and I explained to Mr. Hunt of my experiences of Hillsborough, as did Dean Harris. I firmly told him that hooliganism played no part in the disaster, and that I saw the police open that gate (Gate C). I explained that the disaster was the fault of the police and not the fans. As I said, "I was there, I saw it all unfold before my very eyes."

Mr. Hunt did seem to listen to us, and he listened to Anne Williams, and her account of the past 22 years of fighting the system, of the injustice, of the cover ups, of the lies, of the myths, of the fabrications. He had a copy of her book in his hand and stated that he had read it and that he was 'incredibly moved' by it all. Not enough though, to offer us some hope for justice. He did offer a full and frank apology, and we were in there for nearly an hour and a half. Anne was persuaded not to take the matter further, as the panel members did promise that all the evidence that Anne had would be put before the independent panel to look through. This includes evidence after the '3:15pm cut off point' adopted by the coroner, Popper. No evidence has ever been heard after 3:15pm, despite some of those who lost their lives living beyond this point, and in Kevin Williams' case up to 4pm. We were both rather dubious, but Anne promised not to take the matter further, such as to the Attorney General to grant a fresh, fair inquest under Section 13 of the Coroners Act, until after the panel had released it's findings. There is, however, a deep rooted mistrust and scepticism regarding the panel as HFH is concerned. The 'terms of reference' do not comply with what we want, demand, and what should have been afforded to us over 20 years ago – JUSTICE. I myself have written to the panel personally, and in fact put a question about evidence after 3:15, to Bishop James Jones, the Bishop of Liverpool, in a radio phone in show. He kind of dodged the question, saying that he 'could not discuss the workings of the independent panel.' You can clearly see why we have all of this deep mistrust and scepticism. It appears that those on the panel only seem to listen to the concerns of one of the groups – the HFSG or Hillsborough Family Support Group. The other two groups, the HJC or Hillsborough Justice Campaign and HFH or Hope For Hillsborough, are never mentioned, never listened to and are completely ignored. To me, this is an absolute and utter disgrace.

We got an apology out of Jeremy Hunt, so I guess you could call that progress, but we got little else. I emailed his office a few days later to thank him for seeing us and apologising to HFH. I also invited him to come along to the Hillsborough Memorial Service in April, but sadly

I got no reply. I guess that meeting that he had with us will have long faded from his memory. It makes you think that you are not people, people who have been denied justice as every turn, but merely a number in his diary and in his mind. This is what we have had to battle against for 23 years.

As the weeks went by, it got nearer to the memorial service. I had attended the 21st anniversary memorial service, as I have previously mentioned. I had gone there alone. It had been a very difficult experience. The 22nd anniversary memorial service would be somewhat different. I would not be alone. I would have the love and support of HFH for a start. This would mean the world to me. I travelled by train and had a bunch of flowers with me that I was to lay at the Hillsborough Memorial at Anfield, together with a poem that I had written. I got off the train at Lime Street. I walked into the city centre, where I saw Dean Harris. He drove us up to Anfield.

It was early, around 11am. I walked to the Memorial, to lay the bunch of flowers and the poem that I had written. There was a time of quiet contemplation and reflection on this morning – the morning on the 15th of April – our darkest day, my darkest day. It had been 22 years since the Hillsborough Disaster, but the pain is still very much raw, the wounds very deep, the emotional scars still very much there. Yet, this was progress. I was able to attend, not only football matches again, but also the memorial services at Anfield. I could do neither for many years.

It was a strange sort of day. At first it was sunny and quite warm, pretty much like the 15th of April 1989. However, it clouded over as the day wore on and became decidedly cooler. A number of us gathered in the Albert pub, opposite the Kop at Anfield. It is a pub that I know well. There were a lot of good people in that pub that day, who came to remember the fallen 96. Anne Williams, who is a true inspiration to me and many other people, her daughter, Sara, Jennifer Barton, Scott Turner, Liam Hamilton (who is actually a Manchester City fan), the Burnley

Reds – Mick, Eric, John and Steve, Amanda Tootle, and many, many more. We were a family in togetherness that day – the RED FAMILY. The previous year, as I have had already stated, I went alone, not knowing anybody, having only just returned to watching football after a long gap of several years. It had been hard to get through that day in 2010. I shivered in fear, hurt and pain. In 2011, it was somewhat different. Yes, the pain was there, the fear was there, the hurt was there, but I did not have to face it alone. Having all these wonderful people around me helped immensely. That is what the RED FAMILY is all about, and why Liverpool fans are the greatest fans in the world.

As the months moved on, I felt that I needed to do more for HOPE FOR HILLSBOROUGH. That is why I decided to hold a fund raising event for my 50th birthday in aid of FOR JUSTICE, the official registered charity for HOPE FOR HILLSBOROUGH. On the 24th of June 2011, in the Parish Hall, Saint John the Baptist Roman Catholic Church, Burnley, we had a fantastic night and raised £600. We held a grand raffle, where Kenny Dalglish and Jamie Carragher each donated a signed shirt. It was a truly wonderful event, and HFH was represented by Anne Williams and Scott Turner.

As the summer moved on, and the new football season beckoned, I finally sought some professional help regarding PTSD – Post Traumatic Stress Disorder. I was pretty sure that I had had this terrible, awful condition since the 15th of April 1989, and this was confirmed by someone within my local NHS Mental Health Team. She was really lovely with me and I thought at long last I was getting somewhere with the terrible illness that has afflicted me for more than 22 years. To be perfectly honest it was a huge weight off my shoulders. I was then to have weekly appointments with a counsellor. However, things did not turn out quite as I would have hoped. The counsellor who I saw just was not right for me, and he certainly did not understand what I felt, what I endured, and how Hillsborough has affected my life for so many years. He denied that having been told that I was suffering from PTSD, that I actually had the illness, even though I may have had 'some of the symptoms.' What I really wanted was a diagnosis of PTSD, and he stated that I could only be diagnosed by a psychiatrist. I wanted a referral, he refused. He stated that I was 'not ill enough.' How the hell did he know how ill I was? I have not been to see him since the first couple of sessions and I contacted my GP about my situation. He has helped me immensely and has managed to secure an appointment with the consultant psychiatrist, even though there will be a 22 week wait. I am waiting for a date for that appointment as I write this.

I am now beginning to move on, after 23 years. The pain is still very much there, the fear, the anger, the resentment, the hurt. Yet, I do believe that I am finally beginning to be able to cope. Anyone who has PTSD will tell how about a deep, inner blackness and darkness in their lives revolving around nightmares, anxiety, panic attacks, cold sweats, paranoia, absolute screaming fear, reliving the event over and over again, low self esteem, no confidence, self denial. One hell of a horrible lethal cocktail.

The Information Commissioner, Christopher Graham, decided that all files relating to Margaret Thatcher and Hillsborough should be released into the public domain. These included discussions in cabinet with her ministers following Hillsborough. The BBC had wanted them released, and Christopher Graham agreed. The Government had 35 days to comply, or 28 days to appeal. This was seen as a significant victory for those of us who have been campaigning for JUSTICE for almost a quarter of a century. A total of 23 years of fighting the system. A system that has continually lied and covered up, made up false accusations, fabricated evidence and created myths as regards Hillsborough. Predictably, the cover ups continued. At almost the last possible moment, in a startling example of total insensitivity, the Government, through the Cabinet Office decided to appeal against the Information Commissioner's ruling.

The usual 'not in the best public interest' stick was waved again. The notion that the Independent Panel, chaired by the Bishop of Liverpool, James Jones, should see them first. Yet, the terms of reference with the Independent Panel as regards the release of documents and files relating to cabinet discussions regarding Hillsborough, did not clearly state that these files would be released into the public domain. More lies. More cover ups. More screwing of the bereaved families and the survivors.

Most recently, it was announced that there would indeed be a debate on Hillsborough in the House of Commons, on Monday 17th October 2011. An online petition which gained more than 130,000 signatures in a matter of a few days, asking for the release of ALL documents relating to the Hillsborough Disaster, meant that a debate could be granted if requested. The Labour MP for Liverpool Walton, Steve Rotheram, a Hillsborough survivor, won the fight for that debate. In an example of amazing poignancy, 96 fellow MP's supported his call. It was interested to see how many Government ministers would actually turn up for the debate. The bereaved families want JUSTICE. The survivors want JUSTICE. The vast majority of the public want JUSTICE. The 96 fully deserve JUSTICE. Was this Government going to deny us once again? Was this Government going to lie yet again? Was this Government going to cover up once more, and sweep everything under the carpet? Sadly, it would not have surprised me one bit. However, we are a tough, resourceful lot. We will not go away, we never have done. Despite all the setbacks, despite all the lies, despite all the fabrications and the myths, despite all the cover ups, despite being treated with absolute utter contempt, we are strong and we continue to be strong. We have been the central part of the most controversial case in the history of the British judicial system. We have been denied JUSTICE at every turn and at every angle. This is, without question, an absolute disgrace and a damning endictment of moral corruption. HILLSBOROUGH – the biggest single miscarriage of justice in the history of the British legal system.

To my absolute shock and surprise, the debate produced a victory for us. To her credit, the Home Secretary, Theresa May, gave us some hope. She stated, in an emotionally charged debate, that all papers should be released pertaining to Hillsborough, so that the bereaved families can get to the truth of what happened to their loved ones. A step in the right direction, and only time will tell if we do indeed get the true facts, and ALL the documents, including cabinet minutes and of meetings that Thatcher had with senior police officers from South Yorkshire Police.

Named & Shamed

Below is a list of people who I hold accountable for Hillsborough, and for the cover ups in government and the judiciary, as well as those who printed shameful lies, who created myths and fabricated evidence relating to the disaster:

MARGARET THATCHER: The former Prime Minister of our nation, who detested Liverpool as a city and its people. She destroyed the manufacturing industries of this country and threw millions on the scrapheap, hated the poor, and created the laissez-faire police state, the 'greed is good' culture and 'I'm alright Jack, sod the rest' philosophy. Her false sympathy following Hillsborough is well known. There were survivors in the Sheffield hospitals, who when they knew of her impending visit, signed themselves out of those hospitals. We also know of her insistence that 'no police officer should be prosecuted over Hillsborough.' An absolute disgrace. If the documents that the Government are trying to withhold do get released into the public domain, then I am sure we will see the true, murky picture of her role in the cover-ups over Hillsborough, which came from the very top.

CHIEF SUPERINTENDENT DAVID DUCKENFIELD: The match commander of the day of the disaster, who lied to save his own skin and preserved his fat pension. It was Duckenfield who was the one held most responsible for the disaster by the Taylor Report. It was Duckenfield who failed to close off the tunnel which led to the central pens – Pens 3 & 4 – where most of the fatalities occurred. It was Duckenfield who lied about the opening of Gate C. He claimed at the time that it was the fans who forced open the gate, when in fact he gave the order for the gate to be opened, after dithering for several minutes. I was right next to that gate and saw it being opened. Later on, Duckenfield admitted that he lied. This too, was mentioned in the Taylor Report. Furthermore, Lord Justice Taylor stated that Duckenfield, in his failure to close off the tunnel was 'a blunder in the first magnitude.'

KELVIN MACKENZIE: The former editor of the S*n 'newspaper' and serial compulsive liar. This is the man who stuck the boot in on the bereaved families, the survivors, and all Liverpudlians, a few short days after the disaster. That vile headline THE TRUTH brought so much hurt and pain to so many people, who were already hurting, were severely traumatised and who were in deep pain. In fact, Mackenzie wanted an even more callously cruel headline – YOU SCUM. These myths and lies of 'fans robbing the dead' of 'fighting with brave cops' of 'urinating on corpses' is so far from the actual truth. The actual truth was that these so-called 'yobs' tried to save lives, rescued the injured and dying and were true heroes that day, whilst these 'brave cops' stood around and did nothing. This is now hard, factual evidence. Yet, Mackenzie shows no remorse, and continues with his evil attacks on the fans to this day, still clinging to pathetic myths and lies.

BERNARD INGHAM: The then Press Secretary to Prime Minister, Margaret Thatcher. His disgraceful slur on Liverpool fans, calling them 'a tanked up mob,' is another example of the lies of Hillsborough. This is a man who was in on the cover up from day one.

DOCTOR STEFAN POPPER: The Coroner of South Yorkshire in 1989. A central figure in the vicious web of lies, deceit and cover ups over Hillsborough. A man who acted in a wicked and callous way, from the very afternoon of the 15th of April 1989. A man who ordered blood-alcohol tests on all of the dead, including young children. The thought being 'if we can prove that alcohol was a major factor we can pin the blame on them and we will be home free.' The fatal flaw was that alcohol was not a major factor, the Taylor Report said as much. Furthermore, the vast majority of those that died at Hillsborough had not been drinking at all, and those that were, a small percentage, had only negligible amounts of alcohol in their bloodstream. Yet, this was only the tip of the tentacle. What followed was evil to the extreme. The identification process in the gymnasium, the vile questioning of bereaved relatives, the picture gallery of dead faces, the statement that 'the body belongs to the coroner now, not you,' all added to the anguish, distress and pain of those relatives. Added to this, Popper was 'perfectly happy' with the way that the identification process was set up and carried out. Even worse was to follow with the inquests – the lies, the cover ups, the way the families and survivors were treated, the obvious bias in favour of the police, witnesses not called, statements changed, evidence suppressed, and of course, the now infamous '3:15pm cut off point' for evidence. All of this under the direct jurisdiction of Popper.

DOCTOR DAVID SLATER: The Rotherham pathologist, and another who was all part of the massive and complex web of the denial of justice. His assertion that all victims were clinically dead by 3:15pm is an absolute lie. Anne Williams can testify to this. His further assertion that Kevin Williams' injuries were the worst of any of the victims at Hillsborough, and his claim that he was blue and bloated, is another lie. He compounded matters by contacting Derek Bruder to get him to change his story. A disgraceful decision and all part of this murky plot.

DETECTIVE CHIEF SUPERINTENDENT STANLEY BEECHEY: This was the man who was put in charge of investigating Hillsborough, despite the fact he was under suspension and investigation. Beechey was the former head of the West Midlands Police Serious Crime Squad, a force and a unit riddled with corruption and controversy. Hardly the ideal force to be asked to investigate Hillsborough. Yet, this was all part of the plan. This complex web of lies and deceit, of covering up and sweeping everything under the carpet. West Midlands Police and the Serious Crime Squad were complicit in the case of the Birmingham Six, and a number of other cases. They were at the centre of a number of complaints regarding forced confessions and interrogations that were nothing short of organised and brutal torture. In charge of the Serious Crime Squad, was Stanley Beechey. It is beyond reason and comprehension why this man was put in charge. Yet, it goes much further and deeper than that. During the sham of the inquests, Beechey was often at the side of the coroner, Popper, acting as a Coroner's Officer. Another disgraceful situation.

GRAHAM KELLY, FORMER CHIEF EXECUTIVE OF THE FOOTBALL ASSOCIATION: Kelly was told the lie regarding Gate C by Duckenfield. Instead of investigating whether or not this was the truth or not, he released this version of lies to the waiting media. It was also Kelly, who kept insisting and pressurising Liverpool to 'play on.' There was no thought for the 96 who lost their lives (at that time it was 95), no thought for the bereaved, no thought for the survivors, or indeed the players of LFC. It was a case of 'we must play these high profile games no matter what.' Sickening. Kelly should also have insisted that SWFC had a valid safety certificate, and then if that did not come into fruition then a new venue should have been selected.

GRAHAM MACKRELL, FORMER SECRETARY OF SHEFFIELD WEDNESDAY FOOTBALL CLUB: He was part of the entourage that inspected the buckled barriers and broken down fences of Leppings Lane. He was part of the cover up. Why did he not, as the man responsible for the overall running of the club and the stadium, not communicate with Duckenfield, and not put back the kick off by twenty minutes or so. Kenny Dalglish referred to this in his autobiography. Mr. Mackrell must hold his hands up to take some blame, as his club, SWFC did not hold a valid safety certificate.

These are the central figures in the cover ups and lies, not forgetting the injustice that surrounds Hillsborough. However, there are others, who through their misguided and mythical opinions, and a nest full of lies, have brought much hurt to the bereaved families and survivors. Without trying to actually take the time and trouble to look at the TRUE FACTS regarding Hillsborough, certain people voiced their prejudicial and unintelligent opinions on the world as regards Hillsborough. The likes of BRIAN CLOUGH, who pointed the finger of blame at Liverpool fans in his autobiography, yet who later apologised for his hurtful remarks. Even his own fans, who adored the man, distanced themselves from him. Others, such as TERRY CHRISTIAN, the self proclaimed 'voice of the Mancs,' who rounded on the city of Liverpool with his disgraceful slur calling Scousers 'people of self pity.' BORIS JOHNSON, the Mayor of London (how the hell he got that job I will never know) rounded on the fans and the city in general with similar remarks, and pointing the blame at Liverpool supporters regarding Hillsborough. Another apology came, yet the hurt was still there. Thankfully, for every Boris Johnson, there is a STEVE ROTHERAM, and for every Terry Christian, there is a BRIAN READE, who back us and support us in our fight.

On internet sites too, you get ill-informed members of the public who voice their opinions about Hillsborough, based on no facts or evidence whatsoever, but on petty hatred and prejudicial views of Liverpool, creating this myth and stereotypical view of Scousers in general. These people usually crawl out of the woodwork around the anniversary to peddle their sick mockery and lies. Yet, they crawl back under the stone from which they came pretty quickly when we, as survivors and bereaved families, point out the true facts to them that we have at our disposal. I have had such run ins myself during the past year. A number of people, devoid of any real intelligence, and lacking factual accuracy and concrete, hard evidence. Some claim to be so-called 'supporters' of other clubs and that 'they know what really happened at Hillsborough.' How do they know? Where is all this evidence? When challenged with the real facts, the true evidence, they either back away or just throw childish insults at you. This happens when such people lose the argument.

There are even examples of people who are 'former Liverpool fans.' I had a confrontation with such a person earlier this year. A man by the name of Mike Slater, who came across all 'intelligent' and said that he 'studied at Oxford.' He went on to say that he 'knew exactly what happened at Hillsborough, as his two uncles had been there. They had told him how ashamed they had been of Liverpool fans, who had killed their own.' How come these people never came forward with this so-called 'evidence' of theirs? How come no other Liverpool fans had criticised their own? How come this 'information' was never placed in the public domain? When I gave Slater all the hard, factual evidence, when I gave him my own true account of Hillsborough, he just came back with the same predictable falsehoods and myths associated with the lies of Hillsborough. Eventually, he crawled back under the stone from where he came.

There must be, however, special condemnation and contempt reserved for one individual, who launched a disgraceful attack on Liverpool fans, survivors, bereaved families and the 96 angels themselves. I am of course, referring to the vengeful smears and slurs online, and the disgracefully vile lies and fabrications of Independent Wiltshire County Councillor, RUSSELL HAWKER, who even today claims that those who fight for JUSTICE, Liverpool fans in general, the survivors, the bereaved families, are 'hooliganism deniers.' It is ABSOLUTE FACT that hooliganism played no part in Hillsborough. Or, are these so-called 'hooligans' the same people who acted as selfless heroes that day? As I have stated in a response to Hawker, I truly believe that he is a 'truth denier.' At times you get certain individuals who cling to discredited myths, proven lies, false misconceptions relating to Hillsborough. Their comments are so wide of the mark they would drop off the end of the world. They do not research Hillsborough properly to get the true picture. Why would they? After all, they cling to pathetic, prejudiced and false interpretations regarding Hillsborough, and the fine people of Liverpool in general. Yet, for all of these people who spout this vile filth, they are heavily outnumbered by the vast majority of this country who firmly believe in the quest for JUSTICE. That support is growing by the day. It is known that something like 90% of the population back the fight for justice. The call for a debate in the House of Commons reached 130,000 signatures with an online petition in a matter of a few short days. That shows the true feeling in this case, and it kind of restores your faith in human nature.

I shall briefly return to Mr. Hawker. This is a man who even the Tories threw out of the Conservative Party. This is a man who likes to court controversy, rather than speaking the truth. This is a man who readily attacks single mothers, the elderly, the disabled, or anyone who does not agree with him. This is a man who holds no credibility whatsoever. Naturally, I have contacted Mr. Hawker about his disgraceful lies regarding Hillsborough, and, predictably, I have not had a response. Clearly, if he had facts, if he spoke the truth, if he had evidence, then he would have written back to me. I think it proves who speaks the truth here.

IN CONCLUSION......

I have finally reached the end of writing this account of Hillsborough, the 23 year long, and continuing fight for JUSTICE, and my own battle with PTSD. This has been very much a personal account, and something which has been very difficult to write. Some might call it a remarkable achievement, but I will let you, the readers, be the judge of that. I am hoping that somewhere in the very near future, JUSTICE will FINALLY be served to the bereaved families, the survivors, and of course, the brave 96 who gave their lives that day, the 15th of April 1989. To wait 23 years, to even get a sniff of justice, and to be denied at every turn, is an absolute disgrace and is totally unforgivable. To be lied to, for evidence to be suppressed, to be coerced and bullied into changing statements, for witnesses not to be called, for the denial of basic human rights, for myths and fabrications to be created, for absolute wicked and evil lies being printed about you, your fellow survivors, the bereaved families and the 96 themselves, for the massive cover up from those in authority, whether they be politicians, judges, lawyers, police forces, pathologists, coroners, doctors, the ambulance service, football chiefs, so-called 'journalists' and writers, is an absolute and utter disgrace. An awful lot of people have an awful lot of blood on their hands, in the BIGGEST SINGLE MISCARRIAGE OF JUSTICE IN THE HISTORY OF THE BRITISH LEGAL SYSTEM.

Written in loving memory of the 96 men, women and children who lost their lives at the Hillsborough Stadium Disaster, Sheffield on the 15th of April 1989

YOU'LL NEVER WALK ALONE

Dedicated to the bereaved families, the survivors, the brave rescuers, the former players and staff of LFC from that day, and anyone who has been affected in many different ways

YOU'LL NEVER WALK ALONE

LEST WE FORGET......

All those, whether they be survivors of Hillsborough, or bereaved relatives of those who lost their lives at Hillsborough, who are sadly no longer with us, but are sharing in the peace of Christ with the 96 angels in Heaven. I would also like to pay tribute to those who found the horrors of Hillsborough too much to bear, and sadly, took their own lives. In many ways, these are the forgotten victims of Hillsborough. Another sad fact is that many hundreds of people have suffered some kind of psychological condition since Hillsborough, with PTSD being the most common illness. This is a terrible condition, often described as a 'silent killer,' Sadly, as far as Hillsborough goes this is frighteningly true.

May all of those who passed away since Hillsborough – REST IN PEACE

YOU'LL NEVER WALK ALONE

Christopher Whittle
A Survivor – Pen 4 Leppings Lane
The Hillsborough Stadium Disaster, Sheffield
15th of April 1989

POST TRAUMATIC STRESS DISORDER:

THE SILENT KILLER

POST TRAUMATIC STRESS DISORDER or PTSD can be readily described as a natural and emotional reaction to an intensely disturbing, shocking or terrifying ordeal. It is a psychological condition that is now quite common, and many army war veterans suffer from it, but also do bereaved relatives and survivors of horrific disasters, such as Hillsborough. The symptoms can be described as wide ranging, that include:

- Nightmares
- Flashbacks
- Irritibility
- Panic Attacks
- Cold Sweats
- Paranoia
- Screaming fits
- Sleeplessness
- Violent outbursts/anger
- Anxiety issues
- Fear and dread
- Deep Depression

- Worthlessness
- Suicidal thoughts

Post Traumatic Stress Disorder occurs when a person or persons are exposed to, or when they witness, an event or situation which is outside the normal boundaries and framework of an everyday occurrence. A situation which would cause deep distress, such as a major disaster, a witnessing of death, or physical violence. Obviously, if someone witnesses much death, in terrifying consequences, such as Hillsborough, that is bad enough – nearly 100 deaths in such an awful way – but then to suffer for over two decades with lies made about you, myths written about you, the finger of accusation pointed at you, when, in reality, you were the victim and not the perpetrator, then that is just too awful to contemplate. Yet, this has happened to me and any many other survivors, and bereaved family members since the 15th of April 1989. For some, it was just too much to take.

The so-called 'UK DISASTER ERA' between 1985 – 1989 claimed a total of 1,062 lives. It is often stated and quoted that for every one death in a major incident, some eight people go on to develop Post Traumatic Stress Disorder. If we were to relate those figures to Hillsborough, then some 768 people have suffered from PTSD since Hillsborough. A shocking statistic. Of course, many will not have been diagnosed and there is nothing to suggest that the figure could not be considerably higher. When you take into account that figure being only of those that were actually at Hillsborough that fateful April afternoon, and if you were add those that were bereaved relatives who had to identify their loved ones in the most appalling manner possible, and those that saw the events unfold on live TV in the Grandstand programme, like my own family, then the figure would probably go well beyond the 1,000 mark. Absolutely shocking.

And what has been done for these forgotten victims? In a professional capacity, not very much. It is so often the case that such victims are told to 'move on' or 'get over it.' When you have PTSD 'moving on' and 'getting over it' is not so easy, if not impossible.

And what of the financial implications surrounding PTSD and indeed, Hillsborough itself?

Another deep controversy ensues. Another accusation is often thrown at us regarding compensation. 'You are only after the money.' If that were true, then the bereaved families and survivors would not have received such a pittance, compared to that of retired policemen from South Yorkshire Police. In my own personal case, I received £4,500 as a survivor. Yet, policemen were awarded over a third of a million pounds. Is that right? It is their job to cope with such disasters, they are supposedly trained for it. We, as football fans, following our team, are not. Yet, we had to cope with it, so why shouldn't policemen? We are not after tons of money. We are after JUSTICE. We are after answers as to why 96 people were sent to their deaths, why policemen literally got away with murder, why they were given huge sums of money, why we have had to live with the horrors of Hillsborough and battle the terrible illness of PTSD.

If one was to look at the symptoms of PTSD, there are six key areas in which the criteria must be met:

1. TRAUMA - The person must be exposed to a traumatic event that will involve actual loss of life or serious injury, or a threat to the physical well being of self or others.
2. INTRUSIVE - The event must be persistently relived by the person
3. AVOIDANT - The person must persistently avoid stimuli associated or linked with the trauma.
4. PHYSICAL - The person must experience persistent symptoms of increased arousal, or an over awareness of the event.
5. SOCIAL - The disturbance must cause significant distress or

impairment in social, occupational, personal or other areas of functioning important to that person.

6. TIME - Any symptoms linked to 2 – 5 must have lasted for at least a month (try 22 years).

When a person encounters such an awful life-changing, traumatic and life threatening situation, the brain sets off a variety of deep rooted emotions, in which it recalls the painful memories of the tragedy (intrusive) and going to severely great lengths to forget it, such as turning away from football for many years in my own case (avoidance). The sufferer will experience extreme mood swings between the two emotions.

Whilst there are many symptoms of PTSD not all sufferers will experience every one. However, each symptom has a list of certain situations which will be easily recognisable by the sufferer:

INTRUSIVE –
Recurrent and distressing recollections
Flashbacks, thoughts, nightmares
Phobias about specific daily routines or tasks, certain events, items and objects
Severe feelings of guilt for having survived

AVOIDANT –
A detatchment and a withdrawal from others, lack of emotion
Avoidance of thoughts or feelings associated with the event
A severely diminished interest in a number of activities

PHYSICAL –
Sleep problems
Hypervigilance

Joint and muscle pain, including chest and stomach issues
Severe nervous feelings

SOCIAL –
Outbursts of anger and/or violence
Increased and severe irritation
Impaired memory
Lack of ability to concentrate
Irrational or impulsive behaviour
Low self esteem/lack of confidence
TIME –
Depression
Anxiety

I can readily admit to having suffered from all of the above, and I still do. It is safe to say that you do take one day at a time, and that you have good days as well as bad days. Hillsborough, which I think about each and every day will stay with me forever. I guess so too will PTSD.

Post Traumatic Stress Disorder really is the 'silent killer,'

HYMNS, POEMS, PRAYERS & SONGS

In this section, I would just like to share with you a selection of my favourite hymns, poems, prayers and songs, written by a variety of people including myself.

HYMNS

The first hymn is a traditional one, often sung at the FA Cup Final. Never was it more poignant than at the 1989 FA Cup Final between Liverpool and Everton, a few short weeks after Hillsborough. It was a baking hot day at Wembley that afternoon and it brought more than a few tears to my eyes. This hymn is often sung at funerals, and it is a very sad song, yet beautiful as well.

ABIDE WITH ME

Abide with me; fast falls the eventide
The darkness deepens; Lord with me abide
When other helpers fail and comforts flee
Help of the helpless, Oh abide with me

Swift to its close ebbs out life's little day
Earth's joys grow dim; its glories pass away
Change and decay in all around I see
Oh thou who changest not, abide with me

I fear no foe, with thee at hand to bless
Ills have no weight; and tears no bitterness
Where is death's sting? Where grave thy victory?
I triumph still, if thou abide with me

Hold thou thy Cross before my closing eyes
Shine through the gloom and point me to the skies
Heaven's morning breaks, and earth's vain shadows flee
In life, in death, Oh Lord, abide with me

Words: Henry F Lyte, 1847 Music: William H Monk, 1861

The next hymn that I have chosen is very much a simple one, and as a practising Roman Catholic it is often sung at Church. It means a great deal to me as it recognises the Most Holy Trinity of Father, Son & Holy Spirit which is central to my own faith.

SPIRIT OF THE LIVING GOD

Spirit of the Living God, fall afresh on me
Spirit of the Living God, fall afresh on me
Melt me, mould me, fill me, use me
Spirit of the Living God, fall afresh on me

Spirit of the Living God, fall afresh on us
Spirit of the Living God, fall afresh on us
Melt us, mould us, fill us, use us
Spirit of the Living God, fall afresh on us

The third and final hymn that I have chosen is very much a personal one, as it was sung as the offertory hymn at my wedding. It is a song of life, and of death, of sacrifice and of hope.

THE SERVANT KING

From Heaven you came, helpless babe
Entered our world, your glory veiled
Not to be served, but to serve
And give your life, that we might live
He calls us now to follow Him
To bring our lives as a daily offering
Of worship to the Servant King

There is the garden of tears
My heavy load, He chose to bear
His heart with sorrow was torn
Yet not my will but yours, He said

This is our God, the Servant King
He calls us now to follow Him
To bring our lives as a daily offering
Of worship to the Servant King

Come see His hands and His feet
The scars that speak of sacrifice
Hands that flung stars into space
To cruel nails surrendered

This is our God, the Servant King
He calls us now to follow Him
To bring our lives as a daily offering
Of worship to a Servant King

So let us learn how to serve
And in our lives enthrone Him
Each others needs to prefer
For it is in Christ we're serving

This is our God, the Servant King
He calls us now to follow Him
To bring our lives as a daily offering
Of worship to the Servant King

POEMS

The following poems are deeply personal, moving and at times, sad reflections written by people with strong connections to Hillsborough, several of which have been written by survivors.

The first one was written by myself, a few months back.

I CAME HOME

A bright, sunny April morn
No breath of wind, no rain, no clouds
Everything seemed to be a perfect world
We set off to Sheffield, for the semi
Back to Hillsborough, when last year was a dream
Same opponents, same ground, same sunny April afternoon
And the Reds were back in town
April 15th 1989
The day that 96 brave souls fell
The day they never returned
But me, I CAME HOME

What was so different to 1988?
Everything seemed the same
No fear, no pain, or so it would seem
Those two words – fear and pain
Say so very much about that April day
Why oh why, did 96 have to die?
96 brothers and sisters
Going to a football match, for goodness sakes
Where you don't expect to fight for life
Survival, it was all about survival

Amidst the raw emotion of death
That April afternoon
When I CAME HOME

The eerie silence of loss of life
Inside those horrible caged pens, as people fell
And that vile stench and smell of death
Awful, unrelenting death
The surge, the crush, the painful chest, breathlessness
The aching back, cracking ribs
That's what hit me that April day
That sunny April day, when so many fell
And some got back up on their feet
Many Reds, just like me
And as I wandered hopeless and scared
On that green Hillsborough turf
I saw the lifeless corpses on the floor
The pain was there, all plain to see
And fans, heroic fans, trying to save their fellow Reds
Did they look drunk?
They didn't to me, that April day
When I CAME HOME

When I CAME HOME in dumbfounded shock
My spirit broken, my mind elsewhere, certainly not there
I thought, you liar, Duckenfield
You lying toad
You told them to open the gate
After all, I saw it, I was there
Save your skin and blame the fans
A big fat pension and interests to protect

96 dead by your own rotten hands
Mackenzie and the SCUM, made up stories, lies and myths
Protect those up high and blame the fans
Not forgetting Popper, that slithering, slimy coroner
Who lied and swept it all away
Identify your dead and then get lost
It's my body now, not yours
Oh, and before I forget, I want blood tests on all of the dead
To prove that they were definitely drunk
Even though they weren't
All of this happened when I CAME HOME

West Midlands Police, the bully brigade
We'll question and interrogate
Our 'true facts' will come out
Help our mates and the coroner of course
Then them Scousers can take the rap
22 years of myths and lies
Cover it up and sod the dead
We don't care if the families are hurt
Because you see, we have too much to lose
The survivors too, what do they know?
They were probably drunk
We've seen it all before
Did they have tickets? Probably not
But wait a minute, the evidence is there
The HSE told the truth of that day
Same numbers of fans in Leppings Lane
Same numbers of tickets sold for that day
I too, was one with a ticket
The day that I CAME HOME

22 years is too long a wait
Too long to defend 96 souls
Too long to keep telling them all of the facts
Because all they have got is myth after myth, and lie after lie
All of this is about one thing
HILLSBOROUGH – the 15th of April 1989
It's about JUSTICE which has been denied
To the 96, the families, and those that survived
Can you imagine the pain you endure?
Day after day, year after year
I've had that myself, many others have too
Since the 15th of April
The day I CAME HOME

By Christopher Whittle

This following poem is written by HOPE FOR HILLSBOROUGH member and justice campaigner, Jennifer Rose Barton:

THE DAY THAT LIVERPOOL STOPPED

We lost our friends that tragic day
A cloud of sorrow came our way
The clouds spelt out in the sky above
A darkness that touched our hearts with love
The worst had come, the place was near
Mersey folk stood still tense with fear
Waiting for the dreadful news
Young and old
No one could choose

Hopelessly trapped
In metal surround
Over so soon
96 found
I know you will worry
When they don't come home
But they know in their hearts
They'll Never Walk Alone

by Jeni Barton – written 16th of April 1989, aged 16

I would like to include a number of poems written by Mike Bartram, a Liverpool fan. Mike has written a number of books of poems, and I include some of his excellent work, by his kind permission.

DEATH TRAP

Hillsborough football stadium, Sheffield, February the 4th 1914
An FA Cup tie took place there, with Wolves being the visiting team
A wall on the kop collapsed, causing fans to fall down onto the terraces below
Not a great start for the stadium, with its brand new kop on show.

75 fans got taken to hospital, though thankfully nobody died that day
Only through such accidents we'll arrive at 'perfection' a local newspaper went on to say
But that 'perfection' had not arrived at Hillsborough some 67 years on
When Wolves were again the visitors, playing against Spurs in '81

No problems to be found on the kop that day, but it was a different story
at the opposite end
Were Spurs fans were seen climbing the fences, probably just seen as a
hooligan trend
But 38 Spurs fans had been injured, resulting in a lengthy Hillsborough
semi final ban
Plenty time then for Sheffield Wednesday to put in place that safety
protection plan

But then 6 years later when Hillsborough again became a semi final stage
More crushing still occurred, in the 1987 version of the Leppings Lane
cage
Then of course it was our turn to visit Hillsborough in 1988 and 1989
Near misses occurred in '88, but the following year the death trap was
fully in its prime

SOUTH YORKSHIRE POLICE

I don't like the police in a certain part of the world, and I don't think that
they like me
It's the way that I talk they probably don't like, it's that scouse accent don't
you see
And I think most coppers in the SYP, would still stand by that liar, their
old retired mate
And still believe his lies that us scousers, were to blame by forcing open
that gate
But the Liverpool fans never to blame, and the police cover up, well that
was fully blown
I bet those coppers truly cursed the day, when the truth finally became
known

And I won't forget in '99, when the police took those flowers right out of our hands
And said that they could be used as missiles, to be thrown down from the stands
I didn't realise to carry flowers in Sheffield, had to be met with police approval
But somehow I think from only scousers that they carry out this weapons removal
A police force who took offence, when our fans complained they wanted satisfaction
'Money grabbing, whinging scouse bastards' was probably their secret in-house reaction
But they paid their own 'distressed' coppers out, no doubt with a knowing smile and a cheeky wink
So I still have no respect for the South Yorkshire Police. And I couldn't care less what they may think.

By Mike Bartram, taken from his book, 'JUSTICE CALL: MY HILLSBOROUGH POEMS.'

THAT FEELING

Do you ever get that feeling, just like the one that I've had today?
That something is eating away at your soul, and then cruelly spitting it away
That feeling that something will eat you up, until it eventually swallows you whole
Well that's the way I feel about justice, and it's a feeling that I can't control
Do you ever feel frustrated, when nothing seems to be getting done?
That everything will soon be discarded, forgotten like a burnt out sun

If you ever get these feelings, then it's time to pull together as one
And fight until we get that justice, cos only then will these feelings be
gone.

SCARS

When the very last flower has wilted, and there's no more petals to drop
Please don't think we don't care anymore, and that all our love has come
to a stop
Some promises may appear to be broken, that seemed unbreakable when
they were made
But our memories will last forever, you're a light that will never fade
And a heart doesn't have to travel, to show how much it cares
And a heart can remain invisible, to all the scars it bears
Scars that run deep with anger, scars that will never fade or heal
Until justice is finally done, and the lies, they can longer conceal.

By Mike Bartram, taken from his book 'HILLSBOROUGH: 20 YEARS
ON.'

The following poem was written by fellow Liverpool fan, John
Lemmon:

DEDICATED TO THOSE MEN WITH IMPOSSIBLE ARMS

The men with impossible arms
Have nothing to fear anymore
They were incredibly brave that sad day
They grew up pretty quickly, that's for sure

Those men with impossible arms
Were only there for the game
They did impossible things
Have never since been the same

Those men with impossible arms
Became heroes to me and to you
They performed unbelievable bouts of heroism
Were called thugs, hooligans, yobs too

The stupid sheep like coppers
Who stood firm as Red fans were dying
"Caused it all" said the filthy rag Scum shite
Didn't worry too much about lying

Those men with impossible arms
Were just so incredibly brave
As we bow down and thank them so humbly
Couldn't save 96 souls from the grave

We owe you all a debt of gratitude
As we sit here and wait for the new season
No need for doubt, guilt or remorse
You did what you did for a reason

The men with impossible arms
Saved many more lives on that day
With their selfless actions and bravery
Gets my Victoria Cross come what may

The victims are not just those who were taken
We are all victims of our own destiny throughout the ages
And those men with impossible arms
Have our everlasting thanks twixt history's immortal pages.

John Lemmon

The following are poems, which I have written over the past couple of years or so:

SHATTERED LIVES

When they waved their loved ones goodbye
On that sunny April day
There was no fear in their eyes
Everything is fine, we'll see them tonight
If only they could have stopped them going
If only they could have actually known
If only….
If only there had not been so many SHATTERED LIVES

A catalogue of disgraceful scenes
96 dead, we know the reasons why
'Open the gate,' was a policeman's cry
But from Duckenfield's mouth came a blatant lie
That is why there were so many SHATTERED LIVES
On the 15ᵗʰ of April 1989

Lines of bodies on the gymnasium floor
'Look at the pictures,' how can anybody be so cold?

'Answer the questions,' about time, tickets and booze
How can these coppers be so cruel?
This was the day when so many horrors did unfold
So many SHATTERED LIVES, their loved ones they just wanted to hold

22 years of hurt and pain
Nobody brought to book over the 96 so horribly slain
Too much to hide, too much to lose
No JUSTICE, no closure, despite all the facts
That's nearly a quarter of a century of downright lies
That's why the families, survivors too
Have had to live with SHATTERED LIVES.

By Christopher Whittle

3:15

A man with no heart and no soul
Who lied and schemed to save his pals
And of the 96 whose dignity he deliberately stole
Can you imagine those grey faces riddled in pain?
Do the tests, Popper did exclaim
On our brothers and sisters who had just been horribly slain

We'll prove that they were drunken Scousers, was their cry
To get Duckenfield and his cronies off scot-free
But we all know that this was blatant lie after lie
Yet Popper had an even more devious plan
The heartless coroner with no shame
They were all dead by 3:15 was his absurd claim
What a lie, what an outrageous sham

Popper the vile and odious toad
Would not allow the truth to be told
Friends in high places, crooked cops from another force
Who fabricated and tortured and lied through their teeth
Beechey's boot boys from the West Midlands lot
Who did not care, didn't even give a jot
They bullied, coerced and changed all the facts
No evidence to be heard in a Sheffield court
We'll hide the truth and get our boys off
Those lying South Yorkshire bastards with arrogant grins

Popper and Duckenfield the connection is strong
Who lied and said that nothing was wrong
They raised a glass down at the Masonic Lodge
Those lying, corrupt bastards
Who covered it all up

By Christopher Whittle

DISASTER DAY: A 21ST ANNIVERSARY POEM

As the cold winter months roll on
The lingering night frosts disappear
I cling to an old red scarf as darkness falls
Then as the early buds of spring arrive
There is something deep in my heart which brings trepidation and fear
A warming April brightness shines
Just like that morning in 1989
The 15th of April is Disaster Day

A day etched painfully on my memory
I was at Hillsborough that day
Pen 3 of Leppings Lane
Which brought much heartache and a lot of pain
The rest is horrific history
On that fateful Disaster Day

The dark tunnel faced me straight ahead
There seemed no other place to go
It was a struggle to stand as I faced the crush
My back ached, my chest could take no more
A few minutes later I fell to the floor
I was lucky, pulled up by one brave Red
If I stayed down I would be dead
That is what happened to me on Disaster Day

The S*n, South Yorkshire Police and Thatcher blamed the Reds
All the lies, cover ups, accusations couldn't break us it must be said
21 years later the fight for JUSTICE still goes on
The light of truth is with us now
The secret documents have been sent
For the panel to read and inspect
This will I'm sure shed new light
At last the families, survivors, are winning this fight
The guilty cowards can hide no more
Mackenzie, Thatcher, Duckenfield, Ingham, Popper and all
Their deluded world will crumble and fall
But what is true and what will be fixed
Is all the fear, anger, hurt and pain
And finally there will be JUSTICE FOR THE 96

On the 15th of April 2010
We will all gather, we will all pray
In remembrance of that fateful Disaster Day

By Christopher Whittle

PRAYERS

As a devout and committed Roman Catholic, prayer is a very important part of my life. I have included several prayers which I feel relevant to tragedy, loss and the quest for JUSTICE. I will begin with a trialate of prayers, first of all, with the prayer that Jesus taught us:

OUR FATHER

Our Father who art in Heaven
Hallowed be thy name
Thy kingdom come
Thy will be done
On earth as it is in Heaven
Give us this day our daily bread
And forgive us our trespasses
As we forgive those who trespass against us
And lead us not into temptation
But deliver us from evil
Amen.

Mary, the Mother of the Church, is very important to us Roman Catholics. Below, is her prayer, which we say every day with devout reverence:

HAIL MARY

Hail Mary
Full of grace
The Lord is with thee

Blessed art thou amongst women
And blessed is the fruit of thy womb Jesus
Holy Mary
Mother of God
Pray for us sinners
Now and at the hour of our death
Amen.

The worship of the Most Holy Trinity – Father, Son & Holy Spirit – is central to our faith. This is said each and every day with this simple but most important prayer:

GLORY BE

Glory be to the Father
And to the Son
And to the Holy Spirit
As it was in the Beginning
Is now and ever shall be
World without end
Amen.

It is very true in my own faith that inner strength is a great source of comfort. The following prayer focuses on inner strength and ability to cope and fight for what is right:

Let me not pray to be sheltered from dangers but to be fearless in facing them
Let me not beg for the stilling of my pain but for the heart to conquer it

Let me not crave in anxious fear to be saved but hope for the patience to win my freedom
Grant me that I may not be a coward, feeling your mercy in my success alone; but let me find the grasp of your hand in my failure.

The following prayer was written by John Henry Newman, a true disciple of the Roman Catholic Church:

Jesu, by that shuddering dread which fell on thee
Jesu, by that cold dismay which sickened thee
Jesu, by that pang of heart which thrilled in thee
Jesu, by that mount of sins which crippled thee
Jesu, by that sense of guilt which stifled thee
Jesu, by that innocence which girdled thee
Jesu, by that sanctity which reigned in thee
Jesu, by that Godhead which was one with thee
Jesu, spare these souls which are so dear to thee
Who in prison, calm and patient, wait for thee
Hasten Lord, their hour, and bid them come to thee
To that glorious home, where they shall ever gaze on thee.

I shall now end with this final prayer, and my favourite prayer that is very personal to me and what has happened to me during my life:

FOOTPRINTS IN THE SAND

One night I had a dream
I dreamed I was walking along the beach with the Lord
Across the sky flashed scenes from my life

For each scene, I noticed two sets of footprints in the sand
One belonging to me, the other to the Lord

When the last scene of my life flashed before me
I looked back at the footprints in the sand
I noticed that many times along the path of my life
There was only one set of footprints
I also noticed that it happened at the lowest and saddest times of my life

This really bothered me and I questioned the Lord about it
"Lord, you said that once I decided to follow you, you would walk with me all the way. But I have noticed that during the most troublesome times in my life, there is only one set of footprints. I don't understand why when I needed you most, you would leave me."
The Lord replied, "My child, my precious child. I love you and I would never leave you. During your times of trial and suffering, when you see only one set of footprints, it was then that I carried you."

SONGS

LIVERPOOL is well renowned as the 'capital of music,' and so it is deeply relevant that several songs should be included in this publication. Furthermore, no other football club in the world has as many songs or chants as Liverpool Football Club – there was even a book of songs published!!!

I would like to start with a song that is not only relevant to Liverpool, but also to the deep tragedy of Hillsborough. It is also true that 'Ferry 'Cross the Mersey' was re-released as a single to raise funds following Hillsborough.

FERRY 'CROSS THE MERSEY

Life goes on day after day
Hearts torn in every way
So Ferry 'cross the Mersey
'Cause this land's the place I love
And here I'll stay

People they rush everywhere
Each with their own secret care
So ferry 'cross the Mersey
And always take me there
The place I love

People around every corner
They seem to smile and say
We don't care what your name is boy
We'll never turn you away

So I'll continue to say
Here I will always stay
So ferry 'cross the Mersey
'Cause this land's the place I love
And here I'll stay
And here I'll stay
Here I'll stay.

By Gerry Marsden

The music scene in Liverpool has grown and developed over the years and owes so much to the 'Merseybeat' and especially to the Beatles – they changed the world in a musical sense. I have always been a big Beatles fan, so I thought it would be appropriate to include one of their many songs. My favourite track is 'IN MY LIFE,' which I find to be sad and uplifting at the same time. It talks of loss and of love, of tragedy, of people no longer with us, and of places changed, and it is a song, which forever touches my heart. It is very, very poignant.

IN MY LIFE

There are place I'll remember
All my life
Though some have changed
Some forever, not for better
Some have gone and some remain
All these places had their moments
With lovers and friends, I still can recall
Some are dead, and some are living
In my life, I loved them all

But of all these friends and lovers
There is no one compares with you
And these memories lose their meaning
When I think of love as something new
Though I know I'll never lose affection
For people and things that went before
I know I'll often stop and think about them
In my life, I'll love you more

Though I know I'll never lose affection
For people and things that went before
I know I'll often stop and think about them
In my life, I'll love you more.

By The Beatles

THE FIELDS OF ANFIELD ROAD is now an iconic song adapted from the Irish ballad THE FIELDS OF ATHENRY, and is sung by the Kop at every Liverpool game, home and away. On the 20th anniversary, the song was released as a single by THE LIVERPOOL COLLECTIVE & THE KOP CHOIR.

THE FIELDS OF ANFIELD ROAD

Outside the Shankly Gates
I heard a Kopite calling
Shankly, they have taken you away
But you left a great eleven
Before you went to heaven
Now it's glory round the Fields of Anfield Road

All round the Fields of Anfield Road
Where once we watched the King Kenny play
And could he play
Stevie Heighway on the wing
We had dreams and songs to sing
Of the glory round the Fields of Anfield Road

Outside the Paisley Gates
I heard a Kopite calling
Paisley, they have taken you away
But you led a great eleven
Back in Rome in '77
And the Redmen they are still playing the same way

All round the Fields of Anfield Road
Where once we watched the King Kenny play
And could he play
Stevie Heighway on the wing
We had dreams and songs to sing
Of the glory round the Fields of Anfield Road

Beside the Hillsborough Flame
I heard a Kopite mourning
Why so many taken on that day?
JUSTICE has never been done
But their memory will carry on
There'll be glory round the Fields of Anfield Road

All round the Fields of Anfield Road
Where once we watched the King Kenny play
And could he play

Stevie Heighway on the wing
We had dreams and songs to sing
Of the glory round the Fields of Anfield Road

All round the Fields of Anfield Road
Where once we watched the King Kenny play
And could he play
Stevie Heighway on the wing
We had dreams and songs to sing
Of the glory round the Fields of Anfield Road

The glory round the Fields of Anfield Road.

by The Liverpool Collective & the Kop Choir

I first made contact with local Liverpool singer/songwriter, Stephen Smith upon the release of the single LIAR, LIAR from his album LAST TRAIN TO NOWHERE. The song spoke of the lies printed by THE S*N. Stephen kindly donated royalties from the single to the three support groups HOPE FOR HILLSBOROUGH, HILLSBOROUGH JUSTICE CAMPAIGN & the HILLSBOROUGH FAMILY SUPPORT GROUP,

LIAR, LIAR

It's a truth that's a lie
It's an anger inside
It's a rage I cannot contain
It's a story to tell
It's a smear to sell
You sold dignity with no shame

Well I for one won't let
Won't let myself forget
I don't buy the S*n
I don't buy the S*n

There's a tear in my eye
96 reasons why
There's a flame that forever burns
There are songs to be sung
They can't change what has gone
I pray one day that JUSTICE will come

And I for one won't let
Won't let myself forget
I don't buy the S*n
I don't buy the S*n

Liar, Liar, Liar, Liar
Liar, liar, Liar, Liar

Well I for one won't let
Won't let myself forget
I don't buy the S*n
I don't buy the S*n

There's a scar in my head
There's a sea that is Red
There's a feeling I can't explain
There's a reason for hate
There's a liar to name
Here's 'THE TRUTH'
You should be ashamed

Well I for one won't let
Won't let myself forget
I never will forget
I don't buy the S*n
I don't buy the S*n

by Stephen Smith

There really is only one place, and one song, where we could possibly end. That is with the world's most famous football anthem and one of the most loved songs in the history of popular music – I am of course talking about YOU'LL NEVER WALK ALONE. When Rogers & Hammerstein penned this song for the Hollywood musical, CAROUSEL, few people could have imagined that it would be adapted by Gerry & the Pacemakers during the height of the Merseybeat era,let alone be adopted by the world famous SPION KOP to become legendary in the world of football circles. But that is exactly what happened. Furthermore, the title of this book, WITH HOPE IN YOUR HEART, is taken from this iconic piece of music. The song brings so much comfort to those affected by Hillsborough and is an inspiration to millions.

YOU'LL NEVER WALK ALONE

When you walk through a storm
Hold your head up high
And don't be afraid of the dark
At the end of the storm
There's a golden sky
And the sweet silver song of a lark

Walk on through the wind
Walk on through the rain
Though your dreams be tossed and blown
Walk On, Walk On
With hope in your heart
And You'll Never Walk Alone
You'll Never Walk Alone
Walk On, Walk On
With hope in your heart
And You'll Never Walk Alone
You'll Never Walk Alone

by Rogers & Hammerstein, 1945
Adapted by Gerry Marsden, 1963

JUSTICE FOR THE 96

YOU'LL NEVER WALK ALONE

HELP & SUPPORT

Below is a list of groups and organisations which offers help and support in a time of need:

THE HILLSBOROUGH GROUPS

HFH - HOPE FOR HILLSBOROUGH
www.hopeforhillsborough.org
Contact: annewilliams@hopeforhillsborough.co.uk

HJC – HILLSBOROUGH JUSTICE CAMPAIGN
www.contrast.org/hillsborough
The Hillsborough Justice Campaign
PO Box 1089
178 Walton Breck Road
Liverpool
L69 4WR
Tel: 0151 2605262
email: hjcshop@tiscali.co.uk

HFSG - HILLSBOROUGH FAMILY SUPPORT GROUP
www.hfsg.net

OTHER SUPPORT GROUPS & ORGANISATIONS

CRUSE BEREAVEMENT CARE
www.crusebereavementcare.org.uk

NO MORE PANIC – PTSD SUPPORT
www.nomorepanic.co.uk

MIND – MENTAL HEALTH SUPPORT
www.mind.org.uk

DISASTER ACTION - MAJOR DISASTER SUPPORT
www.disasteraction.org.uk
email: pameladix@disasteraction.org.uk

BIBLIOGRAPHY

Bartram, Mike *Hillsborough 20 Years On* Countyvise, 2009
Bartram, Mike *Justice Call* Countyvise, 2009
Buckley, Monsignor Michael **The Catholic Prayer Book** Darton, Longman & Todd, 1999
Kinchin, David *Post Traumatic Stress Disorder: The Invisible Injury* **Success Unlimited, 2005**
Scraton, Phil **Hillsborough: The Truth** Mainstream Publishing, 2009
Taylor, Right Honourable Lord Justice **The Hillsborough Stadium Disaster: Interim Report** HMSO, 1989
Taylor, Right Honourable Lord Justice **The Hillsborough Stadium Disaster: Final Report** HMSO, 1990
Williams, Anne **When You Walk Through The Storm** Mainstream Publishing, 1999

OTHER SOURCES

Granada Television/Jimmy McGovern, **Hillsborough** Granada TV, 1996
Hillsborough Justice Campaign Website **www.contrast.org/hillsborough**
The Guardian **Keith Twitchell** Guardian Unlimited, 27th October 1999
Nicola McMillan & Jim Sharman **Hillsborough: Contexts & Consequences** hfdinfo.com

Lightning Source UK Ltd.
Milton Keynes UK
UKOW06f2328040516

273594UK00017B/361/P